CIVIL WAR GENERATION

A Strategic Guide to Overcoming the Battles Threatening This Generation's Destiny

AZAEL NUÑEZ

AZAEL NUÑEZ

English Standard Version (ESV)
The Holy Bible, English Standard Version. ESV® Text Edition: 2016. Copyright © 2001 by Crossway Bibles, a publishing ministry of Good News Publishers.
Amplified Bible (AMP)
Copyright © 2015 by The Lockman Foundation, La Habra, CA 90631. All rights reserved.
The Message (MSG)
Copyright © 1993, 1994, 1995, 1996, 2000, 2001, 2002 by Eugene H. Peterson
Holman Christian Standard Bible (HCSB)
Copyright © 1999, 2000, 2002, 2003, 2009 by Holman Bible Publishers, Nashville Tennessee. All rights reserved.
Twenty-First Century King James Version (KJ21)
Copyright © 1994 by Deuel Enterprises, Inc.
Robert Greene's "The 33 Strategies of War." https://www.businessinsider.com/33-strategies-of-war-you-should-apply-to-everyday-life-2012-5#amidst-the-turmoil-of-events-do-not-lose-your-presence-of-mind-4.
Statistics by World Health Organization (WHO)
Statistics by Abort73.com
US Census Bureau statistics
Refinery29.com
Life Way Research 2015
The national fatherhood initiative of 2016
Kingdom Man; by Tony Evans.
Copyright © 2012, published by Lifeway house.
Cover credit: Ismael Paramo
Copyright © 2020 AZAEL NUNEZ
All rights reserved.
ISBN: 9781702405188

CIVIL WAR GENERATION

ACKNOWLEDGMENTS

First and foremost, I give all glory and honor to my Lord and Savior, Jesus Christ. Without Him, this book would not have been possible. I am deeply grateful for His guidance and grace throughout this journey.

To my wonderful wife, Yaneidy Nunez, thank you for your unwavering support and for allowing me the countless hours needed to complete this project. Your patience and love have been my foundation.

To my father, Angel Nunez, who is now with the Lord—your legacy of faith lives on in me. To the entire Nunez family, I am grateful for the spiritual heritage I have inherited, which has been the bedrock upon which I build.

Special thanks to my mentors, David Snyder, Jorge Sepulveda, and Yoeli Sepulveda, for pouring into me during the early days of my ministry. Your belief in me when I struggled to believe in myself has made all the difference.

To my dear friend, Sarah Shoecraft, thank you for your help in editing this book and for your continued encouragement.
I would also like to extend my heartfelt gratitude to my spiritual father, Mark Vega, for your constant support and for inspiring me to push forward when challenges arose.

Finally, to every person who has had an influence on my life, thank you. I am honored to have crossed paths with you, and I am a better person because of your impact. This book is a testament to the many hands that have shaped me along the way.

CIVIL WAR GENERATION

CONTENTS

ACKNOWLEDGEMENT

INTRODUCTION

1	THE GENERATION	1
2	THE PROMISE OR THE PRESENCE	11
3	UNYIELDING FAITH	25
4	THE PHARAOHS OF TODAY	33
5	I AM REMNANT	42
6	THE COST OF THE ANOINTING	52
7	STEWARDS OF GRACE	65
8	MOTHERS OF BREAKTRHOUGH	79
9	RESTORING THE FATHERS ROLE	89
10	CALLED TO DELIVER	97
11	AGENTS OF CHANGE	106
12	UNLEASH YOUR POTENTENTIAL	117

AZAEL NUÑEZ

INTRODUCTION

CIVIL WAR

YOU ARE THE ANSWER TO OUR GENERATION

As I update this book, it has been exactly seven years since I first found the courage to write it. Today, the message within these pages is more relevant than ever. In 2024, our society and world stand at a crossroads, surrounded by chaos, turmoil, and affliction. Yet, in the midst of it all, Jesus remains the answer to a world in desperate need of hope. The Holy Spirit impressed upon my heart on October 17, 2024, to update this book, saying, "This message is for such a time as this."

Consider these sobering statistics: According to Abort73.com, over 150 million babies have been sacrificed at the altar of abortion in America. 31 million Christians did not vote in the last election choosing to remain silent against such wicked times. When young people attend secular colleges, 80% do not return to the church. Twenty-four million children—one out of every three—live in father-absent homes, a crisis recognized by 90% of American parents. We are facing a spiritual battle, a war between a godly and ungodly generation. Yet, God has called a remnant to rise in these last days, standing for His Kingdom in the darkest hours of our society.

Generations may come and go, but the Word of God endures forever. This book, Civil War Generation, is about the generations who fought for truth. In the past, God's people knew Him personally, but this new generation struggles to stand firm. They know about God, but they don't know Him as the God of miracles, power, forgiveness, and salvation. They are unaware that He offers life in abundance.

In this book, you will find a battle plan to fight the spiritual forces attacking this generation and the institution of the family. You will discover the root of the problem in every generation and encounter the identity and tools God has given you to be the answer for this time. Through these pages, may you awaken the calling within you, seek your God-given purpose, and rise to declare that the glory of the Lord shall cover the earth. It's time to fight back.

God heard their groaning, and he remembered his covenant with Abraham, Isaac, and Jacob.
EXODUS 2:24 ESV

AT WAR!

When you see the title of this book, you might assume I'm referring to the Civil War of 1861—but not exactly. The current scenario we face today bears a striking resemblance to the spiritual and cultural battles of that era. I want to examine the stages our generation has gone through, which can be likened to a modern-day civil war of values. Today, we are experiencing a religious and cultural war, as two distinct generations clash over the direction of our society.

On one side, there is the Godly Generation, those who uphold biblical values and walk under the banner of Jesus Christ as their Commander-in-Chief. They fight to preserve truth, morality, and faith in a world increasingly hostile to these principles. On the other side, we face the Ungodly Generation, influenced by woke ideologies that promote a redefinition of morality. This group fights to normalize sin, dismiss traditional values, and spread darkness, all while presenting themselves as champions of progress and enlightenment.

We see these conflicting values play out in today's culture—whether it's the erosion of the family structure, the confusion surrounding identity and gender, or the growing hostility toward biblical truth. Woke ideologies encourage a worldview where anything goes, pushing moral relativism and rejecting the authority of God's Word. Yet, as Peter warned in his time, this same message echoes in our society today: "They promise them freedom, while they themselves are slaves of depravity" (2 Peter 2:19). The battle for the soul of our generation is at hand, and we are truly at war—not with flesh and blood, but with spiritual forces that seek to distort God's truth.

And Peter solemnly testified and continued to admonish and urge them with many more words, saying, "Be saved from this crooked and evil generation!"
ACTS 2:40 ESV

Peter's message to his generation was clear: **We are at war**—living amidst chaos and an evil generation. His words were a call to wake up, stand firm, and remember the spiritual battle raging around them. If Peter were alive today, his message would be just as relevant. He would still be urging the generation of today to recognize the moral decline and spiritual darkness, calling us to turn back to God, rise above the chaos, and be saved from the corruption that surrounds us. His words echo through time, reminding us that the battle we face is as real now as it was then.

Fight the good fight of faith [in conflict with evil]; take hold of the eternal life to which you were called, and [for which] you made the good confession [of faith] in the presence of many witnesses.
1 TIMOTHY 6:12 AMP

Despite the ongoing, subtle battle surrounding us, we often take it lightly or ignore it altogether. But when we truly look at what's happening in the news, movies, music, politics, the education system, and even the financial sector, it becomes clear—we are at war. But who are we fighting? It's a culture war, pitting biblical values against the rising influence of woke ideologies. These ideologies often promote moral relativism, the rejection of absolute truth, and the normalization of behaviors that go against God's design.

One side, the Godly Generation, seeks to proclaim the Good News of the one true God, whose arms are outstretched, ready to save a dying world. On the other hand, the Ungodly Generation promotes lawlessness—encouraging the pursuit of power, lust, promiscuity, and a life free from consequences. They push ideologies that reject God's authority, elevating atheism, and self-serving desires. These opposing forces are fighting for the future of society, each asking: Who will win this war? Which set of values will prevail?

This battle isn't just ideological; it's also seen in the struggle over freedom of religion and freedom of speech. The Godly Generation boldly declares the name of Jesus, offering hope and salvation. Meanwhile, the Ungodly Generation demands political correctness, discouraging public expressions of faith to avoid offending others.

We see this battle manifesting in the fight over same-sex marriage, with one side striving to uphold God's original design for marriage—between a man and a woman—while the other pushes to redefine marriage altogether.

In the education system, the clash is just as fierce. The ungodly forces seek to indoctrinate children with values that reject God and His ways, while the Godly Generation fights to raise up children who follow the God of Abraham, Isaac, and Jacob, the foundation upon which this nation was built.

This is a war between good and evil, one that operates in the flesh but has deep spiritual roots. As the Apostle Paul reminds us:

Finally, be strengthened by the Lord and by His vast strength. Put on the full armor of God so that you can stand against the tactics of the Devil. For our battle is not against flesh and blood, but against the rulers, against the authorities, against the world powers of this darkness, against the spiritual forces of evil in the heavens.
EPHESIANS 6:10–12 ESV

This book is not a battle plan designed to teach us to hate the ungodly generation. On the contrary, it serves as an inspiration to encourage and equip the Godly Generation, reminding us that our victory comes only through selfless love. As we lovingly serve one another, following the example of our Heavenly Father, we must also be committed to praying for those who persecute us. The question we must ask ourselves now is: Can we end this generation's civil war and still bring unity through the power of the blood of Jesus, who died for all generations? This book calls us to love, not division, knowing that true transformation comes from Christ's sacrifice and love for all.

CHAPTER 1
THE GENERATION

"Eventually that entire generation died and was buried. Then another generation grew up that didn't know anything about God or the work he had done for Israel."
JUDGES 2:10

"To be prepared for war is one of the most effectual means of preserving peace."
GEORGE WASHINGTON

There's a story about a small English village that had a quaint chapel, its stone walls draped in ivy. Above the entrance arch, the words "WE PREACH CHRIST CRUCIFIED" were inscribed. For generations, godly men stood behind that pulpit and faithfully preached the message of Christ crucified. But as time passed, the ivy grew, slowly covering the last word, until the inscription simply read: "WE PREACH CHRIST." The next generation did just that—they preached Christ, but as an example, a humanitarian, and a wise teacher, rather than the crucified Savior. Eventually, the ivy grew further, and the inscription was reduced to: "WE PREACH." The generation that followed did just that—preaching economics, social issues, and book reviews, but not the message of Christ crucified.

This reflects the stage we find ourselves in today. Our political landscape is increasingly divided, and the church often remains silent. Yet, the spiritual direction of a nation, a state, and even a local town begins with the Local Church. When the church fails to speak out against laws and ideologies that contradict the Word of God, such as abortion, same-sex marriage, and woke ideologies, spiritual strongholds gain control over our cities. The church must boldly proclaim Christ and stand firm on biblical truths.

Today, many churches seem to have forgotten the original message. There is an emphasis on appearance—ripped jeans and tattoos being associated with anointing—and a tendency to compromise truth in the name of relevance. Rebellion is celebrated as freedom, but in reality, rebellion brings bondage to the soul. Sin is no longer called sin but rather a "symptom" to be excused. The current generation, much like the one described in Judges 2:10, knows about God but lacks a personal relationship with Him. They have lost sight of His miracles, power, and forgiveness.

DO NOT FIGHT THE PAST

"Don't fight the past, but wage war to move forward; do not dwell on what you're not, but focus on who you are in Christ."

This principle, commonly known in military terms as the "Guerrilla War of the Mind," is vital for believers. The enemy often uses our past to condemn us and distract us from God's purpose. But if we choose not to fight the past and instead focus on moving forward in Christ, we will experience victory. True freedom comes from living in the future that Christ has for us, not from dwelling on past failures. Sin should never be viewed as a license to continue in bondage, but through Christ, we are called to live in the abundant life He provides.

> *When you eat and are satisfied, build attractive houses and settle in, see your herds and flocks flourish and more money comes in, watch your standard of living going up and up—make sure you don't become so full of yourself and your things to the extent that you forget God. The God who delivered you from the Egyptian slavery and from your past, the God who led you through that vast and fearsome wilderness, in adversity, he gave you victory. The God who gave you water gushing from a hard rock when you were thirsty. The God who gave you manna to eat in the wilderness, something your ancestors had never heard of, to grant you a taste of the hard life, to test you so that you would be prepared to live well in the days ahead of you. HE provided when you had not a dime in your pocket. Look at the reason why there are contention and welfare all around you. See why it is so hard to follow the one whom you Love.*
> DEUTERONOMY 8 MSG

So now I say, I will not drive them out before you, but they shall become thorns in your sides, and their gods shall be a snare to you.
JUDGES 2:3 ESV

WHY DID GOD LEAVE THESE NATIONS AROUND ISRAEL?

Why would God allow the surrounding nations to remain among the Israelites? What was the purpose of this, especially when He had promised to be with them and deliver them? The truth is, deliverance comes at the cost of battle. The greater the battle, the greater the deliverance, and with that deliverance comes a greater responsibility to maintain it. This was the challenge faced by the new generation of Israelites—they didn't know how to hold on to the victory their forefathers fought for. It became their responsibility to defend what had been won.

In the same way, it is up to us today to help usher in the next generation of "Joshua's," helping them cross over from ignorance and lack of understanding of God's Word into a deep relationship with Him. I feel God calling me more than ever to dedicate the rest of my time to helping this next generation—Gen Z, Gen X, and beyond—encounter His truth. I refuse to leave them behind simply because they "don't get it." I see the potential for God to use this generation powerfully for His glory, and while I still have breath, I will seek God's strategy to reach them.

Israel did not fall into apostasy because they forgot—they fell because sin causes forgetfulness. Sin blinds both those who see and those who do not. This generation must understand what God desires from us. If we, as pillars of our generation, collapse, the next generation will collapse with us. God is calling for a generation to turn to Him, to humble themselves and pray, so that He can be their God. It grieves me to see that the "unchurched" and "churched" generations look so similar. God called us to be light in the darkness, not to become the darkness in order to shine. Jesus commanded us to shine our light, and darkness will flee.

Regardless of your age, as a disciple of Jesus, you carry the responsibility to see this generation saved by His wonder-working power. Imagine how different the world would look if every believer truly knew the ways of God and His miracle-working power!

A LIFE-SAVING ENCOUNTER

I remember one mission trip in Costa Rica during Bible college. I was evangelizing in a park when I met a young man who was homeless, struggling with suicidal thoughts, and overwhelmed by sin. As I shared the gospel with him, he kept saying, "I don't deserve Jesus' forgiveness. I've done too many bad things." I invited him to a service that night and prayed God would soften his heart. That night, he came to the service, responded to the altar call, and accepted Jesus as his Savior. He said something afterward that changed my perspective forever: "Had you not come to the park, I would have taken my life. Now, because of the hope in Jesus, I want to live!"

This is the power you hold as a conqueror in Christ. It's not enough to simply exist in this generation—you must impact those around you.

THE MORAL DECLINE OF ISRAEL AND OUR GENERATION

Israel's downfall began when they started worshiping the gods of the Canaanites, especially Baal and Ashtoreth, gods associated with fertility and sexual immorality. Similarly, in today's culture, people trade their bodies for fleeting attention. Though it may look different, the underlying issue is the same.

THE CHARACTERISTICS OF A CROOKED GENERATION (JUDGES 2:10 ESV)

1. **Friendship with the World:** Israel became friends with the Canaanites, allowing them to lead instead of influencing them toward God (James 4:4).

2. **Love for the World:** They embraced the Canaanite culture, adopting its values (1 John 2:15).
3. **Conformity to the World:** Instead of transforming their environment, they conformed to it (Romans 12:2).
4. **Complacency:** After Joshua's generation passed, they no longer sought God (Judges 2:7).
5. **Apostasy:** They stopped worshipping God and turned to idols.
6. **Loss of Spirituality:** The heart of God was no longer within them.
7. **Tolerance of Sin:** They lost their sense of purpose and conviction, tolerating what God called sin.

THE PATH TO SPIRITUAL DECLINE

Complacency leads to a lack of accountability, which gives birth to apostasy and results in spiritual lawlessness and tolerance of sin. These signs of spiritual decline plagued Israel and are now attacking our generation. Scripture warns us that in the last days, people will become "lovers of themselves." We see this everywhere today—people are more concerned with appearance than with eternity.

But God is calling this generation to be more than just another generation that comes and goes. If we cry out to God for this generation, we will see Jesus lifted high and lives transformed. Men, women, young people, and children will confess by faith that Jesus is Lord.

THE GENESIS GENERATION

God said let us make man in our image [replica].
GENESIS 1:26 AMP

"AS HE IS, SO ARE WE IN THIS WORLD."

The first generation, Adam and Eve, were created as the exact image of the Father. From the beginning, Satan has relentlessly tried to destroy this knowledge, attempting to erase God's image from creation. But despite his efforts, he has not and will not succeed. The Bible tells us that from the time of Seth, Adam's son, through every generation, there have been men and women who desired to know and serve God. Let's take a brief look at some of these individuals who chose to trust God, took risks in their faith, and changed the course of history.

- **Enoch** walked so closely with God that he was taken up and was no more.
- **Abraham** believed God, and it was credited to him as righteousness.
- **Jacob** wrestled with God and was renamed Israel, forever changing his identity.
- **Moses** may have been unqualified by the world's standards, but God chose him to lead His people out of bondage, even allowing him to see God face to face.
- **Joshua** led the Israelites to inherit the Promised Land because he chose to believe God in the wilderness.
- **Gideon**, through obedience, became Israel's deliverer.
- **Ruth**'s persistence led to her redemption, and she became the great-great-grandmother of Jesus.
- **Samuel** dedicated his life to God from childhood and became the advisor of a nation.
- **David** sought after God and was called a man after God's own heart.
- **Job** served God faithfully through severe trials and was blessed with twice as much after proving his faithfulness.
- **Daniel** refused to bow to the world's patterns and became a symbol of God's power and protection.
- **Jesus** came to seek a generation that would pursue Him in spirit and in truth.

WHAT WILL BE SAID ABOUT OUR GENERATION? LET US BE THE GENERATION THAT:

- Walks with God like Enoch.
- Lives not for ourselves, but for the Kingdom of God.

- Believes God like Abraham and is called righteous.
- Wrestles with God for His blessings, as Jacob did.
- Sees God face to face, as Moses did.
- Possesses the Promised Land, like Joshua.
- Is made up of mighty men and women of courage, like Gideon and Deborah.
- Anoints the next generation, as Elijah did with Elisha.
- Seeks God's heart, like King David.
- Declares, "Though He slay me, yet will I trust Him," like Job.
- Refuses to bow to Babylon, standing defiant like Daniel and the Three Hebrew Boys.

Let us be the JESUS Generation!

"The only thing necessary for the triumph of evil is for good man to do nothing"
Edmund Burke

Imagine if our generation united. God says, "Nothing will be impossible." If we valued each other's lives, regardless of skin color, and came together as one across our nation and the world, we wouldn't see the rise of hatred, division, or brokenness like we do today. There would be no ISIS, no riots, no abortions, and no racism. The evils of this world are a direct result of the division that exists within our generation. Though I speak of an ideal world, it's important to recognize that we are living in times foretold—where the love of many has grown cold, as Scripture says, and where division and confusion reign, fulfilling the word of God.

As a generation, we must reject selfishness, care for our neighbors, and rise above the chaos. Confusion has crept into our society because of the divisions that surround us. Although many seem unaware of it, confusion leads to hatred, jealousy, and a desire for what is wrong over what is right. Who is fighting for the children dying in the streets? Who is fighting for the fatherless, the homeless, and the voiceless? Our world is in turmoil, and it's time to wake up. Like in the book of Genesis, when the people were building the Tower of Babel and were scattered by confusion, so too are we today—divided and distracted from what truly matters. We've stopped fighting for truth, for justice, for the ones we love. As Edmund Burke famously said, "The only thing necessary for the triumph of evil is for good men to do nothing." The Godly Generation must rise. We can no longer afford to sit on the sidelines. We must stand up with the Spirit of God and shine our light in the darkness. You have been created for such a time as this.

As you read this book, I pray that no matter where you find yourself in life, you will give these words a chance to speak to your heart. Keep an open mind, whether you are a believer or someone who doesn't know God. My desire is for this book to resonate not only with Christians but also with those who have yet to discover the truth about God and His love.

In this book, I invite you to journey with me as we explore questions about your purpose, the world around us, and the systems that shape our lives. My goal is to bring a renewed sense of awareness to every person who reads these pages. We are created for far more than just a career, task, or assignment. Regardless of your current situation, there is more to life than what meets the eye.

You are filled with untapped potential. Your best days are not behind you—no matter your age—and they aren't even just ahead of you. Your best days are now. Now is the time to break free from what holds you back. Now is the time to pursue your dreams and discover your purpose. Now is the time to build your life on the unshakable foundation of Jesus Christ.

God is not waiting to do the impossible in your life—He already did it. He sent His Son to die for you, to pay the price for your sin. Now, He's waiting for you to respond. You might think, "I've tried everything, even God," but have you truly surrendered? Have you given Him the wheel of your life? It's time to come home. Whether you are a successful person who seems to have it all or someone who feels rejected and lost, this book is for you. It's been designed to alert you: We are at war.

I hope that as you turn each page, you won't feel condemned but instead inspired. I pray that every word will bring you peace and strength to walk in truth. Life is filled with seasons, and at the peak of each one, the decisions you make will shape your future. But above all, always choose truth over facts. God's truth, found in His Word, will bring healing to every hurt you've experienced. My prayer is that the words written here will awaken your passion, ignite your desires, and set you on fire for righteous living like never before.

THE CHALLENGE
#SHARE A VERSE WITH A NON-BELIEVER

So will my word be which goes out of my mouth;
It will not return to me void (useless, without result),
Without accomplishing what I desire,
And without succeeding in the matter for which I sent it.
ISAIAH 55:11 AMP

God's Word is powerful, and He promises that when it is spoken, it will not return empty—it will accomplish exactly what it was sent to do. The challenge for you today is simple: share a Bible verse with someone—a non-believer or a friend who may not know the Lord. This isn't about creating an uncomfortable moment, but about offering hope in a world full of sadness. There is nothing more powerful or encouraging than God's Word.

I've experienced this firsthand. While traveling on a bus, I felt led to take out my Bible and read. The Lord put it on my heart to share a specific verse with the man sitting next to me:

"For I know the plans and thoughts that I have for you," says the Lord,
"plans for peace and well-being and not for disaster to give you a future and a hope. Then you will call on me, and you will come and pray to me, and I will hear [your voice], and I will listen to you. Then [with a deep longing] you will seek me and require me [as a vital necessity] and [you will] find me when you search for me with all your heart."
JEREMIAH 29:11–13 AMP

As I shared this verse, I could see how surprised and encouraged he was by the message of hope and purpose from God's Word. You never know how much someone might need that very encouragement.

As you go about your day, I encourage you to listen to the Holy Spirit. Let Him guide you to someone who could use a word of encouragement. The more you allow yourself to be led by the Spirit, the easier it becomes. Choose today to be led by the Spirit!

CHAPTER 2
THE PROMISE
OR
THE PRESENCE

These are the nations that the Lord left in the land to test those Israelites who had not experienced the wars of Canaan. He did this to teach them how to war the generations of Israelites who had no experience in battle. So the people of Israel lived among the Canaanites, Hittites, Amorites, Perizzites, Hivites, and Jebusites, and they intermarried with them. Israelite sons married their daughters, and Israelite daughters were given in marriage to their sons. And the Israelites served their gods.
JUDGES 3:1, 5–6 ESV

Few men have virtue to withstand the highest bidder.
GEORGE WASHINGTON

THE BATTLE OF GENERATIONS
The scripture in Judges 3:1, 5-6 (ESV) provides insight into why God left certain nations among the Israelites, stating:

"These are the nations the Lord left to test those Israelites who had not experienced the wars of Canaan...The Israelites lived among the Canaanites, Hittites, Amorites, Perizzites, Hivites, and Jebusites. They intermarried with them and served their gods."

This passage reveals why so many failures occurred within the generations of Israel and why, even today, we face the consequences of decisions made by our forefathers. God left these ungodly nations to teach His people how to fight spiritual battles, as those who had not experienced war needed to learn how to stand firm. Similarly, in our generation, very few are standing strong in prayer or holding God's standard high. The battles God saw back then are the same we face today in our society.

In the following chapters, we will explore six distinct **Generations** that represent the spiritual giants we must confront today. These enemies are not just external but are woven into our culture, blinding many to the true spiritual battle. Entertainment, distractions, and confusion dominate, making it difficult for people to focus on the real fight at hand. I believe God called me to write this book to expose Satan's schemes and awaken a Godly generation to rise and fight.

"Every generation faces a giant that God has already defeated."

This chapter will begin with the **Canaanites**, the first enemy God mentioned in His Word. Israel had to learn how to engage this generation. The Canaanites were financial giants, driven by greed and lust for material wealth. The Hebrew word for Canaan ("Kna'an") translates to "humiliated" or "disgraced," and since they were traders, it also came to mean "shameful merchants." Israel was confronted with a culture solely focused on material gain, with no fear of God, worshipping the gods of greed and lust. Their standards were nonexistent—they were willing to lie, cheat, and destroy for riches.

Fast forward to today, and we can clearly see that the spirit of the Canaanites is alive and well in the 21st century. Greed and lust dominate every level of society, from Wall Street to Hollywood, from politicians to the lower-income communities. This spirit is not just in the world; it has infiltrated the church as well, where some see God only as a source of material blessings. After receiving what they've prayed for, many lose interest in a personal relationship with Him until they need something again. But God desires for us to love Him for who He is, not for what He can give us. Are we in love with His presence or only the things He provides?

IDENTIFY YOUR ENEMY

In warfare, the military uses a tactic known as the Polarity Strategy to identify their enemy. In this strategy, soldiers are trained to recognize signs and patterns that reveal the target they are fighting against. Once identified, they declare war. The same principle applies in our spiritual lives. Recognizing the true enemy often gives us the purpose and motivation to fight back and remove what shouldn't be in our lives.

The challenge for us is this: are we focusing on material blessings, or are we seeking God's presence above all else? The enemy wants to paralyze our purpose by keeping us worried about unanswered prayers. This tactic keeps us distracted from the real battle—against the greed and materialism that has infiltrated our hearts. Like Moses, we must seek God's presence as the most precious treasure in our lives. When we do, the desire for material things fades, and we find true contentment as sons and daughters of the Most High God.

In this battle of generations, we must rise as warriors of faith, recognizing the spiritual giants in our midst and standing firm in God's truth. Only then will we experience true victory.

And Moses said to Him, "If Your presence does not go [with me], do not lead us up from here."
EXODUS 33:15 AMP

In Exodus 33:15 (AMP), Moses said, *"If Your presence does not go [with us], do not lead us up from here."* Moses knew that the presence of God was more valuable than the promises He could give. Imagine for a moment if salvation didn't come with all the benefits we often seek—healings, blessings, restoration. What if all we had was Jesus Himself? Would that be enough for us, especially in a world driven by materialism? My father once taught me that desiring God above His promises is crucial because only Jesus truly satisfies. This is the lesson the three Hebrew boys understood when faced with a fiery furnace.

They boldly declared:

If it be so, our God whom we serve is able to rescue us from the furnace of blazing fire, and He will rescue us from your hand, O king. But even if He does not, let it be known to you, O king, that we are not going to serve your gods or worship the golden image that you have set up!
DANIEL 3:17–18 ESV

Their focus was on God Himself, not just what He could do for them. Today, many people desire the benefits of salvation but neglect the responsibility of cultivating a deep relationship with God. It's a problem we see not only in the world but also within the church. We want the blessings, but not the commitment to God's presence.

But the [Holy] Spirit explicitly and unmistakably declares that in later times some will turn away from the faith, paying attention instead to deceitful and seductive spirits and doctrines of demons.
1 TIMOTHY 4:1 AMP

The generation we live in often pursues the "blessings" of God without seeking Him. As 1 Timothy 4:1 (AMP) warns, *"In later times, some will turn away from the faith, paying attention to deceitful spirits and doctrines of demons."* Many will fall away because they desired the promises more than His presence. When those promises seem delayed, they turn to other things for fulfillment. This is why we see so many people leaving the church today—disappointment in unmet expectations blinds them to the true treasure: God's presence.

One day, in prayer, God asked me a simple but profound question: *"Do you want My promises or My presence?"* It struck me deeply, making me realize that sometimes we can turn the promises of God into idols. We can become so focused on what He gives that we forget the true prize—Himself. This is the same encounter Moses and the Israelites had when they were invited into God's presence at Mount Sinai. The people were afraid and chose to distance themselves, asking Moses to speak to God on their behalf while they waited for the promises.

This kind of thinking is prevalent today. We often leave the "spiritual" work to pastors, leaders, or the most devoted person in our household. But the presence of God is not something casual—it's precious and powerful, and comes with responsibility. God will not pour out His presence on those who won't honor it.

Today, many want the "promised land" but want nothing to do with God's presence. We must realize that God's presence holds the power to transform our lives. In His presence is fullness of joy (Psalm 16:11), and it is His presence that will lead us through the deserts of life, not just the promises of material blessings.

God desires an intimate relationship with each of us. His promises, such as in Exodus 23:25-27 (AMP), are not just about provision and protection but about walking hand-in-hand with Him: *"You shall serve the Lord your God, and He will bless your bread and water... I will fulfill the number of your days."* His presence is the key to experiencing His promises, and it is our responsibility to be good stewards of both.
In the end, the choice is clear: seek God's presence, and everything else will follow.

THE CHOICE

One day in prayer, the Lord asked me, *"Do you want My promises, or do you want My presence?"* Without hesitation, I responded, *"God, I want both, because I know that is what You desire for me."* But then He asked again, *"What if you had to choose between the two? Which would you choose?"*
In that moment, my heart sank. I realized that, at times, we can turn God's promises into idols, prioritizing what He can give us over the beauty of His presence. You might wonder, *How could that happen?* I believe it's something we all must guard against—seeking the blessings more than the Blesser.

As you read through the rest of this chapter, my prayer is that your heart will be opened to this revelation: we must long for God's presence above all, for His presence is far greater than any promise we could ever receive.

Moses and the Israelites faced this very same choice. Their story reveals the significance of choosing God's presence over everything else.

> *of lightning and the sound of the trumpet and the smoking mountain; and as they looked, the people were afraid, and they trembled [and moved backward] and stood at a [safe] distance. Then they said to Moses, "You speak to us, and we will listen, but do not let God speak to us or we will die." Moses said to the people "Do not be afraid; for God has come to test you, and so that the fear of Him [that is, a profound reverence for Him] will remain with you, so that you do not sin." So the people stood at a [safe] distance, but Moses approached the thick cloud where God was.*
> EXODUS 20:18–21 AMP

God Himself came down to speak to His people, extending an invitation to experience His presence. But the Israelites were so afraid that they wanted nothing to do with Him. Their eyes were fixed on the promise of the Promised Land, not on the presence of God. They told Moses, *"You speak to God and we will wait,"* essentially saying, *"You spend time in His presence, and we will stay here at a distance."* This is one of the saddest moments in the relationship between God and His people.

"The presence of God is not casual; it is costly."

It breaks my heart to see that even today, many young people, families, and marriages treat God in the same way. They leave the responsibility of connecting with God to the most spiritual person around, while they wait from a distance. But God longs to invite each one of us into His presence. The tragedy is that many treat it as something casual, not realizing the precious value of being with God. The Israelites told Moses to speak to God on their behalf because they understood that being in His presence comes with responsibility. God doesn't offer His presence lightly—He offers it to those who honor it.

Today's generation often desires the Promised Land without wanting to be near the God who provides it. They want the benefits without the relationship. But God's presence brings power. In His presence, the desire to sin fades away. In His presence, there is fullness of joy (Psalm 16:11). This is why seeking His presence is so essential for our lives.

God's heart for Israel, and for us today, is to build an intimate relationship with Him. He desires that we seek Him more than the blessings He can give. In Exodus 23:25–27 (AMP), He promises to bless and protect those who serve Him: *"You shall serve only the Lord your God, and He shall bless your bread and water. I will also remove sickness from among you... I will send my terror ahead of you and throw into confusion all the people among whom you come."*

God made it clear—He will guide us to the Promised Land by His own hand. This is the goodness of God for you and me today. Whatever promise He has spoken over your life, He will fulfill it if you remain in His presence. He will protect you through the deserts and trials on your way to the promise. Today, God declares over you: *"I WILL be with you."*

Every promise of God comes with a responsibility. They are precious gifts placed in our hands. Now, it is up to us to be good stewards of both His promises and His presence.

ARE YOU TIRED OF WAITING?

We need to settle this truth in our hearts: God's timing is always perfect. In Exodus 32:1 (AMP), when the people saw that Moses delayed coming down from the mountain, they gathered before Aaron and said, *"Come, make us a god who will go before us. As for this Moses, the man who brought us up from the land of Egypt, we do not know what has become of him."* The people became restless and impatient, allowing their focus on the Promised Land to turn into idolatry.

When you become tired of waiting on God, it's a sign that the promise has become more important to you than God's presence. In our world today, we see the same thing happening—ministries, callings, dreams, and God-given assignments that fall apart because people get tired of waiting and take matters into their own hands. Just like the Israelites, they say, *"We don't know where this man Jesus is, so let us create our own way forward."*

Moses, however, had a heart that burned for God's presence daily, not just for the destination. He wasn't consumed by getting to the Promised Land but by being in God's presence every step of the way. With God's presence, you don't need to wait to arrive at the Promised Land to feel fulfilled—He can come into your life every day as He promised.

When we focus more on the material rewards of following God rather than His presence, we risk becoming spiritually stiff-necked and blind to the things of the Spirit. This is a dangerous place for any believer to be—caught between the decision of whether to sacrifice the promise for His presence or to choose His presence over the promise. God tests not just our actions but the motives of our hearts, as the Psalmist reminds us.

In Psalms 106:20-21 (AMP), it says, *"They exchanged [the true God who was] their glory for the image of an ox that eats grass. They forgot God their Savior, who had done such great things in Egypt."* The same tactic Satan used with Israel, he still uses today with believers—shifting our focus from God's presence to the material things we desire. This isn't done through obvious temptations but by luring us with what our hearts already desire—just like how the Israelites focused on the Promised Land rather than God Himself.

When Moses was on the mountain with God, shouldn't the people have been worshiping at the foot of the mountain? Instead, they grew impatient. An idle mind became the playground for the enemy, allowing him to plant thoughts of creating an idol in the meantime. If they had been focusing on worship, they wouldn't have fallen into idolatry. When our thoughts shift from Jesus to the things of this world, we invite the enemy to shift our focus from God's presence to the pursuit of His promises.

In Exodus 32:23 (ESV), the people said to Aaron, *"Make us a god who will go before us; as for this Moses, we don't know what has become of him."* God had already promised them in Exodus 23 that He would take them to the Promised Land if they obeyed His commandments. But instead of trusting in God's timing, they wanted a quick fix. They wanted to reach the promise without the responsibility of walking with God.

The heart of this chapter is to remind us that God is not withholding His promises from us. He is not holding back anything good. The issue is that we have shifted our focus from loving His presence, which ultimately brings about the promises, to simply pursuing the benefits. Don't allow impatience to drive you away from God's presence. The promise is coming, but it will only be truly fulfilling if you stay rooted in His presence.

WILL GOD GRANT HIS PROMISE WITHOUT THE PRESENCE?

Yes, He Will, and I Can Prove It

In Exodus 33, we find a moment similar to Exodus 23, where God had promised to go with His people. However, after testing their hearts, God saw that they were more in love with the Promised Land than with His presence. His response was heartbreaking.

"The Lord spoke to Moses, saying, 'Depart, go up from here, you and the people whom you have brought from the land of Egypt, to the land which I swore to Abraham, Isaac, and Jacob, saying, 'To your descendants I will give it.' I will send an Angel before you and drive out the Canaanite, the Amorite, the Hittite, the Perizzite, the Hivite, and the Jebusite. Go up to a land flowing with milk and honey; but I will not go up in your midst, because you are a stiff-necked people, and I might destroy you on the way.'" (Exodus 33:1–3 AMP)

Due to the people's disobedience, God decided to send an angel to lead them instead of going Himself. But Moses, refusing to accept this, sought God's presence. He knew the importance of God's presence and would not settle for anything less.

Many of us, in a similar situation, might be content to move forward without God's continual presence, simply because we're more focused on the prize than on Him. But Moses' first reaction was to insist on God's presence. He declared: *"If Your presence does not go with us, do not lead us up from here"* (Exodus 33:15 AMP).

"The Promised Land is temporary, but God's presence is eternal—it carries you into glory."

Moses was willing to leave behind the Promised Land if it meant losing God's presence. He understood that while the promise might be for a season, the presence of God would sustain him for life and into eternity. Unfortunately, the rest of the Israelites didn't grasp this. Out of 2 million people, only Moses and Joshua experienced God's presence firsthand. The rest stood at the doors of their tents, watching from a distance as Moses met with God face to face (Exodus 33:8–9).

They could have had the same experience, but they delegated the responsibility to Moses and Joshua. This is why they were the only two carriers of God's presence among millions. If you want to bring God's kingdom to earth, like Moses and Joshua, you must pay the price. The church cannot wait for heaven; we must bring the reality of heaven to this broken world.

We need God's presence again—His presence is what changes our culture, government, cities, and laws. The sickness of sin in this generation can only be healed by the presence of God. Our youth, who are lost in drugs, gangs, and other destructive paths, need God's presence. Marriages on the brink of divorce, parents making difficult decisions, and Christians who have drifted away need the presence of God to transform their lives.

My own life was changed in a single moment in God's presence. On December 31, 2010, I was at my lowest point—addicted, lost, and filled with shame. But when I heard the message of Jesus' love, despite all I had done, His presence filled the room, and everything changed. The Greek word for "presence" literally means *the face of God*. When we seek God's presence, we come before Him just as we are, and He meets us with grace. Proverbs 18:16 says, *"A gift opens the way and ushers the giver into the presence of the great."* The greatest gift we can offer is the surrender of our hearts, and when we do, it ushers us into the presence of greatness—into the presence of God Himself.

That day, God's presence filled the void in my heart, changing me from the inside out. Ever since that encounter, I have never been the same. I don't serve God for what He can give me—I serve Him because I love Him with all my heart. I am a seeker of His presence, and without it, I cannot live.

PROPHETIC MESSAGE TO THIS GENERATION

One morning while praying for this generation, the Lord spoke to me, saying, "The church is becoming more focused on the benefits they can get from Me than being consumed by My presence. Many seek My promises, but few desire to dwell in My presence. In the West, people are trapped by society's idea of the 'American Dream,' forgetting that I am their source. A time is coming when I will expose those who follow Me for blessings rather than out of love for My presence. I am coming back for a church that loves Me for who I am, not just for what I can give."

We need to understand the times we are living in. Just as Israel wanted to enter the Promised Land but had little regard for God's presence, today's church reflects the same attitude. This is not only a spiritual issue; it affects our personal lives, decisions, and even the political landscape.

Recent elections in the U.S. reflect how deeply this divide runs, with many Christians swayed by the prevailing "woke" ideologies that contradict biblical values. Today, in 2024, we may be facing one of the most pivotal elections in our nation's history. America, a beacon of liberty and democracy for the world, is at risk of losing its foundation if biblical values are sidelined. While God is sovereign, as Romans 13 reminds us, it is crucial for believers to vote in alignment with His Word. Billy Graham once urged us "to vote the Bible". Yet, over 51 million Christians don't see the importance of voting; they don't believe in the election of the president of a nation. For that reason, biblical values decline because the Church is supposed to make their vote count as well as let their voices be heard, but if we are quite them we are letting the woke agenda in this nation win, leading to the decline of biblical values.

America has long been viewed as a "second Israel," as many prophets have declared. What we are witnessing today is the reaping of what has been sown. Just as Israel asked for a king to be like other nations, rejecting God as their ruler, we too have placed more trust in political leaders and systems than in God's leadership.

"But their demand displeased Samuel when they said, 'Give us a king to judge and rule over us.' So Samuel prayed to the Lord. The Lord said to Samuel, 'Listen to the voice of the people regarding all that they say to you, for they have not rejected you, but they have rejected Me from being King over them.'"
1 Samuel 8:4–7 ESV

This generation has also rejected God's kingship, turning to political parties for solutions rather than seeking His presence. Many Christians are more concerned with social and economic policies than with righteousness and truth. God spoke to Samuel, and He's speaking to us today: the people are reaping the consequences of rejecting God's leadership.

If the ungodly agenda continues to prevail, the church will face persecution like never before. The same spirit that ruled Babylon is creeping into our society, seeking to silence those who stand for righteousness. As in the days of Shadrach, Meshach, and Abednego, believers may face persecution for standing firm in their faith.

But here's the challenge: it's not too late to seek God's presence. Amid the cultural and political turmoil, God is looking for those who will choose His presence over His promises. In the last days, the true followers of Christ will be distinguished from those who only seek material benefits.

The church needs to rise, be vigilant, and fight the spiritual battle not with worldly weapons, but by seeking God's presence and being led by His Spirit. Our prayers, our faith, and our actions must be rooted in a deep relationship with God, not just in pursuit of His blessings. Only then will we be prepared to face the trials ahead and fulfill our calling in these last days.

The Challenge
#Tell Someone About What You're Trusting God With

And we know [with great confidence] that God [who is deeply concerned about us] causes all things to work together [as a plan] for good for those who love God, to those who are called according to His plan and purpose.
ROMANS 8:28 AMP

In a world filled with tragedy and uncertainty, people are searching for answers. Where do we turn when everything seems to be falling apart? Perhaps you know someone who's been diagnosed with cancer, lost a loved one, gone through a divorce, or is struggling with a difficult breakup. People today aren't looking for a flawless church; they are looking for real people who have found hope, even in the midst of their struggles.

We, as believers, have discovered that the only true source of hope is Jesus Christ. However, many around us are still seeking that peace. This is a call to share your own journey—your struggles, yes, but more importantly, how trusting in God has made all the difference. When you lean on Him, you'll find that He's the one fighting your battles.

One of the greatest needs of our generation is to show others how to cast their burdens onto Jesus. Many people in your life may be unaware that Jesus can be their peace in the midst of their storm. How can we expect them to find peace if they've never heard of the Prince of Peace? Every victory you've experienced is a testimony that God wants to use to inspire others. Be the one who shares His peace and guides others to victory in Jesus' name.

CHAPTER 3
UNYIELDING FAITH IN A WORLD OF OPPOSITION

For God did not give us a spirit of timidity or cowardice or fear, but [He has given us a spirit] of power and of love and of sound judgment and personal discipline [abilities that result in a calm, well-balanced mind and self-control].
2 TIMOTHY 1:7 AMP

Nothing is more harmful to the service, than the neglect of discipline for that discipline, more than number, gives one army superiority over another.
GEORGE WASHINGTON

The second group God allowed to remain among the Israelites to teach them warfare were the **Hittites**. Known for their cruelty and terror, their name in Hebrew (chathath) means "terror." They inhabited the hill country around Hebron. The Hittites were the same people who sold Abraham the cave where he buried his wife, and David later encountered them when he committed adultery with the wife of a Hittite.

Today, we face similar challenges that Israel encountered with this enemy. The devil, though unable to create, excels at manipulating those who open the door to him, especially through fear. Fear has paralyzed countless Christians, despite the fact that God has given us a spirit of boldness. Many forget that "greater is He who is in us than he who is in the world."

"The spirit of boldness God gave this generation often lies dormant under the weight of fear."

However, Daniel and the three Hebrew boys in the Bible show us how to defy fear. Daniel, despite being a young man taken into captivity, made up his mind not to defile himself with the king's food or wine (Daniel 1:8 AMP). He remained steadfast in his faith, refusing to compromise despite his circumstances. This teaches us the importance of being bold in our faith, even when the world tries to instill fear and pressure us to conform. Just as Daniel was tested, every believer will face moments where their faith is put to the test.

Daniel's story begins with him and three of his Hebrew brothers—Hananiah, Mishael, and Azariah—being taken into captivity in Babylon.

Among these were Daniel, Hananiah, Mishael, and Azariah, from the tribe of Judah. The chief official gave them new names: to Daniel, the name Belteshazzar; to Hananiah, Shadrach; to Mishael, Meshach; and to Azariah, Abednego(Daniel 1:6–7 ESV).

These four young men were without physical defect and had devoted themselves to following God's wisdom. They were knowledgeable, perceptive, and capable of serving in the king's palace. But they were taken to Babylon—a city that symbolized a kingdom of darkness, where everything contradicted God's commandments. Similarly, today's society mirrors the Babylonian system. Just as the Babylonians tried to indoctrinate Daniel and his friends with their language and culture, today we face influences that pressure us to conform to ungodly standards. Washington's political agenda, for example, often runs contrary to God's will.

One of the Babylonians' first steps was to immerse these young men in their culture and teach them the Chaldean language and literature—an attempt to reshape their identities and make them forget the God they served. The pressure to conform was intense, but Daniel and his friends, rooted in their faith, resisted. This resonates with the pressures we face today in education, media, and politics. Our current education system, much like Babylon's, often teaches ideologies that are contrary to biblical values, replacing truth with worldly philosophies.

In addition to indoctrinating them, the Babylonians attempted to erase their God-given identities by changing their names. In biblical times, names held great significance, reflecting one's character and calling. Daniel, meaning "God is my judge," was changed to Belteshazzar, meaning "Bel protect his life" (Bel being a Babylonian idol). Hananiah, meaning "the Lord shows grace," was renamed Shadrach, meaning "command of Aku" (the moon-god). Mishael, meaning "Who is like God?" was changed to Meshach, meaning "Who is like Aku?" And Azariah, meaning "the Lord is my help," became Abednego, meaning "servant of Nebo" (the god of death). This attack on their identity aimed to disconnect them from their faith and heritage.

This tactic is not unlike what we see today, where the identity and values of God's people are constantly under siege. Our names may not be changed, but the world seeks to redefine who we are and what we believe. Like Daniel and his friends, we must be defiant in the face of this pressure, standing firm in our identity in Christ and resisting the temptation to conform to a world that does not honor God. We are called to rise as a generation of conquerors, to be ambassadors of Christ, and to refuse the lies that attempt to reshape our beliefs and identity.

THE ANACONDA PLAN

"Today, you can starve your fears and feed your faith by declaring war on the enemy once again."

During the Civil War, General-in-Chief Winfield Scott crafted the "Anaconda Plan" in May 1861. The Union (the North) targeted key southern ports and commerce hubs, effectively choking the South's economic stability until it collapsed, forcing them to surrender. Similarly, the enemy devised a plan against Daniel and his friends, stripping them of their homeland and forcing them into a new culture, with the intent to choke their identity and security. The enemy's goal was to brainwash them, making them forget who they truly were.

In today's world, the enemy's "Anaconda Plan" is at work, particularly through our education system. In 2024, the greatest battle for our generation is an unseen giant, one that aims to indoctrinate our children with ideologies that stand against God's truth. We're witnessing attempts to normalize same-sex marriages, allowing children under 18 to make their own decisions in changing their body parts choosing a lifestyle of transgenderism as early as the age of 12! What in the world are they thinking? These irreversible decisions about their bodies are a sad truth in our society and even introducing sexual education to children as young as 6 steers them toward a life of fornication. The leaders we don't vote for are the ones making these life-altering decisions for us. Our democratic system is designed so that our voices can be heard and our choices respected. But when we remain silent, we allow those we did not choose to make decisions on our behalf, like passing amendments that let children decide if they want to be a boy or girl based solely on their feelings. This is beyond comprehension! We need revival in our land, revival in our schools, and revival among our governmental leaders. The time to stand for truth and godly principles is now! It's heartbreaking to see our nation, one I love deeply, bow to this agenda that threatens the spiritual future of our most vulnerable—our children. We need Holy Spirit-filled teachers and leaders in our schools. The enemy is stealing our children's God-given futures right before our eyes, and we cannot remain silent.

Just as the enemy used the "Anaconda Plan" against Daniel, he uses the same tactic today—isolating us, making us feel alone, squeezing out our hope and faith. But we can reverse this strategy. Today, you can starve your fears and feed your faith, declaring war on the enemy and reclaiming your peace, purpose, and identity in Christ.

The enemy's ultimate aim is to steal your identity. Whether through abuse or suffering, he wants to take what God has purposed in you. John 10:10 says that the enemy comes to steal, kill, and destroy, but Jesus came to give life abundantly. If we allow him, the enemy will distort our identity—turning what God has made worthy into unworthy. The kingdom of Babylon, with all its counterfeits, is the same today. It represents the enemy's attempt to replace the true with the false. That's why it's crucial to recognize and resist the enemy's attacks, reclaiming our God-given identity and purpose.

ARE YOU A CONFORMER OR TRANSFORMER?

In today's society, where it often feels like the world wants nothing to do with God, we must still live by the principles outlined in Romans 12:1-2. The Apostle Paul urges us to be transformed rather than conformed to the world. He writes:

"Therefore, I urge you, brothers and sisters, by the mercies of God, to present your bodies [dedicating all of yourselves, set apart] as a living sacrifice, holy and well-pleasing to God, which is your rational (logical, intelligent) act of worship. And do not be conformed to this world [any longer with its superficial values and customs], but be transformed and progressively changed [as you mature spiritually] by the renewing of your mind [focusing on godly values and ethical attitudes], so that you may prove [for yourselves] what the will of God is, that which is good and acceptable and perfect [in His plan and purpose for you]."
(Romans 12:1-2 AMP)

Transformation requires us to actively engage with and challenge the systems and values of this world. In our present day, this includes the laws and policies being passed that contradict God's principles. If we, as followers of Christ, remain silent, we allow others to dictate the moral direction of our society. This includes issues such as laws around gender identity, education, and moral values. It is not enough for us to merely exist as Christians in a world that resists God; we must get involved in the decisions being made that shape our society. Voting, advocacy, and public engagement are all essential steps in being transformative agents of change.

Conformers are those whose lives are shaped by external pressures, while transformers, like Daniel and his friends, stand firm, being shaped by God's power within them. These men refused to be changed by Babylon's ungodly culture; instead, they influenced those around them and remained faithful to God. They didn't rebel but remained steadfast and committed to the truth.

Here are steps to becoming a transformer:

1. **Seek God First**: Set yourself to seek the Lord. As Proverbs 4:23 says, "Keep your heart with all diligence, for out of it spring the issues of life." A heart that loves and trusts in the Lord can discern right from wrong, helping you make godly choices.
2. **Honor Your Body**: Remember that your body is the temple of the Holy Spirit, so honor it by living in a way that reflects God's holiness.
3. **Respect Authority**: Even when you disagree with those in leadership, as Proverbs 16:7 says, "When a man's ways please the Lord, He makes even his enemies be at peace with him." Respect for authority, combined with obedience to God, leads to peace.
4. **Engage in Society**: Be involved in shaping culture. Advocate for godly values and defend your faith. As 1 Peter 3:15 urges, "Be ready to give an answer to anyone who asks about the hope within you."
5. **Endure Trials**: Don't run from trials. They are tools God uses to mold your character. The wisdom and strength gained from trials enable you to influence the world around you.

By engaging in societal transformation—through prayer, advocacy, and action—we can resist the ungodly pressures of this world and be part of the solution that brings God's kingdom values into every sphere of life.

THE CHALLENGE
#TAKE ACTION IN SHAPING OUR SCHOOL SYSTEM FOR JESUS!

One of the most powerful ways we can make our voices heard and protect the future of our children is by getting involved in the laws and policies that directly shape their lives, especially in the school system. As believers, we are called to not only live out our faith but to stand up for what is right, ensuring that our children are raised with biblical values in a world that often contradicts them.
Here's how you can take action:

1. **Attend School Board Meetings**: Start by attending your local school board meetings. This is where decisions are made that impact the curriculum, policies, and culture of your children's education. Be present and listen to what's being proposed, and don't be afraid to speak up when something contradicts your biblical beliefs.
2. **Run for School Board**: If you're passionate about protecting the values taught to our children, consider running for a position on the school board. You don't need to be a politician—just a person with a desire to make a difference and ensure that biblical principles are upheld in your local school system.
3. **Petition and Advocate**: Partner with other like-minded parents and community members to petition against laws or policies that oppose biblical values, such as unbiblical gender ideology or teachings that go against God's design for family and morality. Use your voice to advocate for the inclusion of moral, biblical principles in education.
4. **Educate Yourself and Others**: Equip yourself with the knowledge of current laws and proposed changes. Share this information with your church community and encourage them to get involved as well. Together, you can be a collective force advocating for godly change.
5. **Pray for Wisdom and Boldness**: Don't underestimate the power of prayer. Pray for wisdom and boldness to speak truth

in love, and for God to raise up more believers to step into positions of influence.

I believe that our schools are one of the most important battlefields for the heart and future of the next generation. Protecting our children's biblical values requires our active involvement in shaping the systems that educate them. Let's rise to the challenge and make our voices heard for God's truth!

CHAPTER 4
THE PHARAOHS OF TODAY

To fear the LORD is to hate evil; I hate pride and arrogance, evil behavior and perverse speech.
PROVERBS 8:13 ESV

I am sure that never was a people, who had more reason to acknowledge a Divine interposition in their affairs, then those of the United States; and I should be pained to believe that they have forgotten that agency, which was so often manifested during our Revolution, or that they failed to consider the omnipotence of that God who is alone able to protect them.
GEORGE WASHINGTON

Pharaohs in ancient times were notorious for their prideful leadership, and although Israel had escaped the land of Egypt, the spirit of pride followed them into their new land. **The Amorites**, one of the enemies God allowed to remain in their midst, represented arrogance and boastfulness. As Amos 2:9 mentions, they were giants in stature, but Israel's true battle was not with their size—it was against the pride that sought to corrupt their hearts. Today, our culture celebrates pride more than ever, particularly when people boast in their achievements without acknowledging God. We see this embodied in events like "Pride Parades," where people boldly declare their identity and lifestyle choices with no regard for divine truth.

But the question remains for the godly generation: Where does our pride come from? Is it based on our own accomplishments, or do we humbly depend on God, giving Him the glory for all we achieve?

We are reminded of the Israelites' condition in Exodus, where a new Pharaoh arose who did not know Joseph. Despite the Israelites being more numerous and mightier, they fell under the rule of the Egyptians because they failed to recognize their strength and identity in God. The same is happening today. The enemy, who is often smaller and weaker, has deceived us into living under his control. The pharaohs of this generation—whether it be pride, secularism, or personal ambitions—have bound us in spiritual slavery. Yet, like the Israelites, we are called to rise up and bring about a new exodus, leading this generation out of darkness and into God's marvelous light.

Let us remember who we are in Christ. The enemy only succeeds when we forget our identity and the strength that comes from our Creator. Let us not be a generation that forgets God's works, but instead, one that rises in faith and humility to break the chains of pride and walk in freedom.

> *And Joseph died; all his brothers, and all that generation. But the children of Israel were fruitful and increased abundantly, multiplied and grew exceedingly mighty; and the land was filled with them.*
> EXODUS 1:6–7 ESV

THE CONTROLLED-CHAOS STRATEGY

"We must infuse the next generation with the prophetic word for their lives."

When a great generation passes away, the door is left open for the next generation to make gods of themselves rather than following the one true God. This is the reality we are witnessing today. Many of us were raised by parents who taught us respect, morality, and how to strive for greatness, but now we are seeing a generation of young people who rebel against authority, drop out of school, and indulge in sinful behaviors. Yet, there is still hope—there are those who remain faithful, following the godly examples set before them. However, we also see new "pharaohs" rising—leaders and influencers who seek to recruit our youth for their own political agendas, steering them away from God's truth.

As followers of Christ, it is our responsibility to equip the next generation to confront the "pharaohs" that will continue to rise after we are gone. We need to apply a strategic, military-like mindset to this spiritual battle. In any war, including a cultural war, speed and adaptability are key. The culture around us is shifting rapidly, and we must respond faster, armed with God's wisdom, before we are overtaken by it. We, along with the help of the Holy Spirit, must train the next generation to stand for righteousness and integrity, even when no one is watching.

It is essential that we impart the prophetic word over their lives and give them a mission to carry forward. They are not merely observers but active participants in the kingdom of God. Their mission is to be the solution to the brokenness and moral decay of this generation. They, like us, must take responsibility and rise to the challenge. Together, we must run the race, shoulder to shoulder.

The new pharaoh in Exodus arose out of fear and hatred for the people of Israel, refusing to honor the covenant Joseph had established. He was determined to oppress the Israelites and maintain control, just as many leaders today fear losing control to outside influences. Pharaoh painted the Israelites as a threat to Egyptian stability and enacted harsh measures to keep them in bondage:

> *Therefore they set taskmasters over them to afflict them with their burdens. And they built for Pharaoh Supply cities, Pithom and Raamses. But the more they afflicted them, the more they multiplied and grew. And they were in dread of the children of Israel. So the Egyptians made the children of Israel serve with rigor. And they made their lives bitter with hard bondage—in mortar, in brick, and in all manner of service in the field. All their service in which they made them serve was with rigor.*
> EXODUS 1:11–14 ESV

Just as Pharaoh sought to control the Israelites through oppression, the enemy today seeks to control and confuse the next generation. But we have the power to break this cycle. It's time to rise and empower the next generation to know their identity in Christ and to stand strong in the face of the world's challenges.

Pharaoh in the Bible was a tool of the enemy, oppressing the people of God and enslaving them, making them feel powerless. Today, the spirit of Pharaoh is alive in our society through various forms of oppression—bondage to sin, depression, secularism, and spiritual warfare. Satan cannot create; he only imitates and manipulates what already exists. His strategy remains the same throughout history: attacking God's people in cycles until they surrender to fear and compromise. Just as Pharaoh's regime oppressed the Israelites, there are "Pharaohs" in today's culture working to suppress biblical values and oppress God's people.

Look at our current society—right from Washington, DC, to local city halls, agendas are being pushed that are aimed at dismantling biblical values. We see woke ideologies trying to redefine morality, passing laws that promote lifestyles contrary to God's word, such as same-sex marriage, gender identity choices for children, and the separation of church and state. These "modern Pharaohs" wear suits and hold positions of power in government, entertainment, and the education system, steering society further away from God. Although some godly leaders hold these positions, we need more who will boldly stand for righteousness.

What we are witnessing today is no different from what happened in ancient Egypt. Pharaoh justified his oppression by portraying the Israelites as a threat to Egyptian society. In the same way, today's culture frames Christians and biblical values as threats to progress, manipulating the masses to suppress the church's voice. But we must remember that in every generation, God raises deliverers—just as He raised Moses—to confront these modern-day Pharaohs and lead His people into freedom.

Why is it so crucial for biblical values to shape our culture and government? Jesus, who operated in the roles of King, Priest, and Prophet, was involved in the political and social affairs of His time. He demonstrated how the kingdom of God intersects with every aspect of life, including governance. As Christians, we are not called to passively accept the decay of our culture but to actively engage in shaping it through biblical truth.

Jesus declared in John 10:10, "The thief comes only to steal and kill and destroy; I have come that they may have life and have it to the full." But so many in this generation believe the first part of that verse more than the second. They are consumed by fear and oppression, just as the Israelites were under Pharaoh. But Jesus came to offer us life, freedom, and victory over sin and oppression.

The Apostle Paul echoed this sentiment when he said, "For sin shall not have dominion over you, for you are not under law but under grace" (Romans 6:14). Yet, many in this generation feel like sin still reigns over them. The teenager struggling with their identity, the single mother in a cycle of abusive relationships, the addict who keeps falling back into addiction—they all believe they are trapped, but that's the lie of the enemy. Pharaoh's oppression has convinced them there is no way out, but God has already prepared an "Exodus" for them.

God's promise is clear—every struggle has an exit. The way out of oppression, fear, and sin is Jesus Himself. He is calling each of us to rise up, break free, and walk in the abundant life He has promised. Just as He sent plagues to break Pharaoh's hold on the Israelites, God will move against anything that stands in the way of His people's freedom. He is calling you to come to Him, lay down your burdens, and find rest in His presence.

"Come to me, all of you who are weary and carry heavy burdens, and I will give you rest" (Matthew 11:28). Pharaoh may have held you in bondage for a season, but Jesus is the one who offers eternal freedom. You are not bound by the sin, fear, or oppression of this world—you are called to walk in the light and freedom of Christ.

The "Pharaohs" of today—whether they manifest in oppressive laws, cultural ideologies, or personal struggles—are no match for the power of God. Just as He led the Israelites out of Egypt, He will lead you out of every form of bondage. Trust Him, follow Him, and you will experience the life He has promised—a life of abundance, joy, and victory.

Pharaoh Versus Moses

Throughout history, there have always been pharaohs who rise to spread darkness, oppression, and destruction. But in every generation, God has also raised Moses-like figures who stand up to bring hope, freedom, and restoration. For example, during the Holocaust, Adolf Hitler embodied the spirit of Pharaoh by mobilizing an entire generation to carry out unspeakable evil. Yet, God raised up a coalition of nations—men and women from all walks of life—who fought to defeat the Nazi regime and bring justice to the oppressed. This wasn't just a military victory; it was a triumph of good over evil.

The pharaoh of racism reared its ugly head during the era of slavery and segregation in the United States and other parts of the world. But God raised a Moses in the form of Dr. Martin Luther King Jr., who, through nonviolent resistance, faith, and love, led the civil rights movement that transformed the nation and inspired the world. Dr. King didn't fight with weapons of hate or division but with the power of love, unity, and God's justice, bringing about the civil rights reforms that changed the fabric of society.

In the same way, the pharaoh of promiscuity and moral decay rose in the mid-20th century, attempting to lead people away from God and deeper into sin. But God raised a Moses in the form of Billy Graham, who, alongside thousands of missionaries, stood up to preach the Gospel to the ends of the earth. Through crusades, media, and personal dedication, they shared the life-changing message of the cross and called people back to repentance, holiness, and relationship with Jesus.

What was the secret behind these men and women who became the "Moses" of their time, standing against the pharaohs of their generation? It wasn't their personal strength, intelligence, or influence. It was their unwavering faith in God, their obedience to His calling, and their willingness to be vessels of His love, justice, and truth in a broken world. Just like Moses of the Bible, these individuals were deeply rooted in God's presence, and it was through His power that they became agents of transformation in their generation.

Now, the question remains: Who will rise as the Moses of our generation? Who will stand up against the modern-day pharaohs and lead people toward freedom, restoration, and the life God intends for them? The call is clear, and God is still looking for those willing to answer it.

A PROPHETIC MESSAGE FOR THIS GENERATION

The Pharaohs of this Generation have come in the disguise of "self-praise." And self-idolatry. The Bible warms us,
For people will love only themselves and their money. They will be boastful and proud, scoffing at God, disobedient to their parents, and ungrateful. They will consider nothing sacred.
2 TIMOTHY 3:2 ESV

These modern-day pharaohs cloak themselves in righteousness but operate as wolves in sheep's clothing. As Jesus said, "Beware of false prophets who come disguised as harmless sheep but are vicious wolves" (Matthew 7:15). Today, pharaohs are advancing secular agendas, using political platforms to stifle biblical values, silence the church, and oppose the Christian faith. But just as in the days of Moses, God is raising up leaders today who will lead an exodus toward righteousness and faith.

This new generation of conquerors must rise up, not with silent submission but with boldness. We must declare the truth of God's Word in every sphere—government, schools, workplaces, and society at large. We will not bow to persecution or be silenced by fear. The prophetic word for this time is clear: the pharaohs of today will rise against God's people, but they will not prevail.

As Moses stood in the gap for Israel, God saw their suffering and remembered His covenant. The Bible says in Exodus 2:23–25, "God heard their groaning, and He remembered His covenant... and was concerned about them." Persecution will come, but it will drive us to call on the name above every name—Jesus. When we cry out to Him, He will hear and deliver us just as He did for the Israelites.

The truth is, we've grown too comfortable with our pharaohs—those sins, systems, and influences that keep us in bondage. But just as Pharaoh couldn't suppress the multiplication of God's people, no force today can stop the growth of God's kingdom. The more the world tries to oppress and silence us, the more we will multiply and flourish. The gates of hell will not prevail against the church of Jesus Christ.

God will part the seas and bring judgment on any force that tries to stop His kingdom from being established. The pharaohs of your past will not keep you from becoming the Moses of this generation. You are called to lead, to set the captives free, and to take this generation into the Promised Land of God's victory and purpose.

One of the greatest dangers to anyone who knows God is to let pride remain unchecked. Pride causes us to set ourselves up as gods and leads us down the path of destruction. This is why our generation is wandering—we are serving the god of "self." But true freedom comes when we surrender our ego and allow the Holy Spirit to lead us. The Holy Spirit is our seal of approval, marking us as sons and daughters of God, and empowering us to rise above the pharaohs of this world. Let us go forth with confidence, knowing that God is with us, and nothing can stand in the way of His purposes for our lives.

THE CHALLENGE
#ASK SOMEONE IF YOU CAN PRAY FOR THEM

And the prayer of faith will restore the one who is sick, and the Lord will raise him up; and if he has committed sins, he will be forgiven. Therefore, confess your sins to one another [your false steps, your offenses], and pray for one another, that you may be healed and restored. The heartfelt and persistent prayer of a righteous man (believer) can accomplish much [when put into action and made effective by God—it is dynamic and can have tremendous power].
JAMES 5:15–16 AMP

The challenge for you today is simple but impactful: pray for someone. Don't just pray quietly in your heart, but approach them and ask if you can pray together. While this may seem difficult for some, trust that if you listen to the Holy Spirit, the result will always be worth it. Jesus said in John 14:12 that we would do even greater works than He did. The prayer of a righteous person is powerful and effective. When prayed in faith and aligned with God's will, it can move mountains.

One day, while I was working as an Uber driver, I picked up a man who was clearly in pain, using a cane and asking to be taken to the hospital. He explained that he had been in a severe car accident that left his ankle dislocated, and he was preparing for surgery. I felt the Holy Spirit prompting me to pray for him. As I did, we agreed in Jesus' name for his healing. This man was a Muslim, yet after the prayer, he thanked me and said he felt peace because of Jesus. As he exited the car, I noticed something miraculous—he was no longer limping, and he had left his cane behind.

You, too, can have moments like this if you allow the Holy Spirit to guide you. Take the step to pray for someone today—you might be the one to lead them to an encounter with the Father.

CHAPTER 5
I AM REMNANT

So too at the present time there is a remnant, chosen by grace.
ROMANS 11:5 ESV
Let us raise a standard to which the wise and honest can repair; the rest is in the hands of God.
GEORGE WASHINGTON

In today's world, we witness a troubling loss of self-control. Whether it's the numerous accusations of sexual misconduct among Hollywood elites or politicians, or the exploitation of women in the workplace, these behaviors are merely symptoms of a much deeper issue—rebellion. This rebellious spirit mirrors the character of the Perizzites, whose name means "rebellion." Their society operated without discipline or boundaries, and when such values infiltrate a culture, especially one that belongs to God, it creates a toxic environment ripe for chaos.

We are seeing the same today. As rebellion thrives, so does the erosion of moral clarity and the rise of societal disorder. A world without boundaries inevitably descends into chaos, but God has given us divine principles and laws, not to restrict us, but to protect and guide us in righteousness. His boundaries keep us safe from the enemy's destructive plans.

"These are the records of the generations of Noah. Noah was a righteous man, blameless in his generation; Noah walked with God."
Genesis 6:9 (AMP)

We are living in a time not unlike the days of Noah. As Allan C. Carlson, a Lutheran historian, has pointed out, statistics reveal the disintegration of our social fabric. From 1960 to 1980, divorce rates in the U.S. tripled. Fertility rates have dropped, and single-parent households have skyrocketed. With marriage increasingly devalued, we are reminded of Aldous Huxley's dystopian prediction: one day, marriage licenses would be sold like dog licenses—valid for only a year, with no restrictions on changing spouses or keeping multiple partners.

While society around us unravels, there remains a remnant, chosen by grace, who stand for God's truth and uphold His design for life, family, and righteousness. As we raise a standard of godly living, the wise and honest will gather. The rest is in the hands of God.

THE '60S: A DECADE OF TRANSFORMATION AND REBELLION

The 1960s marked a pivotal moment in history, where cultural and societal norms began to shift dramatically. This decade is often seen as the beginning of the progressive movement that we still see rippling through society today. Critical decisions made during this era radically altered what was once considered "normal," especially regarding morality and authority.

One of the most notable changes was the rise of the countercultural "free love" movement, which challenged traditional values around relationships, sex, and family. With the introduction of the birth control pill, sexual promiscuity increased, and the fear of consequences like pregnancy lessened. As a result, the concept of love and commitment began to erode. Homosexuality also started to gain legal ground, and drug use, especially hard drugs, became rampant. This was a time when rebellion against authority—what I like to call the "Spirit of Rebellion"—took center stage. People didn't want to be told they were wrong or that there were consequences for their actions. They wanted to live for themselves, without accountability to moral standards.

While figures like Dr. Billy Graham and Dr. Martin Luther King Jr. were fighting for justice and equality, much of society was distracted by their pursuit of personal pleasure. This divide between righteousness and unrighteousness was evident, as some fought for civil rights, while others embraced a lifestyle of rebellion and self-indulgence. The 1960s were not just a time of civil rights movements and war in Vietnam—nearly 47,000 American lives were lost in that conflict—but also a time when moral degradation began to take hold.

SEEING THE WORLD YOUR OWN WAY: THE COUNTERCULTURE OF THE '60S AND '70S

One group that encapsulated the anti-authority sentiment of the era was the "Diggers." This group, part of the larger hippie movement, operated out of California and believed in the rejection of materialism. They would steal to provide food, which they then gave away for free. Their requirement for receiving this food was simple: you had to walk through a six-foot-tall frame. This was a metaphor for seeing the world their way—a world where everything was free and you could shape reality to fit your desires. They encouraged others to adopt their ideals and even gave new members a necklace as a symbol of their shared worldview.

This kind of free-spirited thinking influenced every part of society, including institutions that were once built upon biblical values, such as Harvard University. Once a beacon of Christian thought, Harvard, like many other academic institutions, became a breeding ground for liberal ideologies in the '60s and '70s. Figures like Professor Gordon Kaufman of Harvard Divinity School began promoting theology that distanced itself from the personal, relational God of the Bible. Kaufman viewed God as merely a symbol, a construct of human imagination rather than an objective, transcendent being. His influence on generations of theologians contributed to the rise of modern liberal theology, which sought to remake God in humanity's image rather than acknowledging the biblical God who reveals Himself.

THE COLLEGE CAMPUS AS A BATTLEFIELD FOR IDEOLOGY

Fast forward to today, and we see the lasting effects of this progressive shift, particularly in our school systems. College campuses, once rooted in biblical truth, have become battlegrounds for ungodly ideologies. In 2024, we've seen college students themselves leading protests, advocating for liberal causes and woke ideologies that run counter to biblical principles. The enemy's strategy has long been to target young people, and just as Daniel and his friends were college-age when they were taken to Babylon, the disciples were chosen to change the world in their late teens into their twenties. How much more is our society today focusing on brainwashing our young adults? This is a prime age for someone to understand their calling and their mission in life. But most of our college-age students are being ravaged by satan's schemes to be directed into living a lifestyle of sin, and sex orientation confusion; today's students are under immense pressure to conform to a world that rejects God's truth. If you did not notice, in 2024, our college campus came out swinging for the fences in protesting liberal ideals that defended unbiblical points of view. This topic of our college campuses being infused with ungodly agenda had been a topic, but in 2024, the students themselves declared a culture war, and many of their stands were to defend diabolical ideologies created in the pits of hell in the name of fighting for a cause.

This is why we must pray for our college campuses, where revival has already begun in pockets across the nation. We need Holy Spirit-filled students, professors, and leaders to stand up for righteousness, turning the tide on campuses and bringing biblical values back into places of influence. Academia will not hold our students in bondage forever; God is raising up a generation that will take their place in government, healthcare, education, and other spheres of influence.

THE PRICE OF REBELLION AND THE CALL FOR REVIVAL

The societal changes of the 1960s were accompanied by movements like "free love," which led to a rise in sexually transmitted diseases and a breakdown of the family unit. AIDS cases surged by 70% during this era. Music, which became the heartbeat of the rebellion, glorified promiscuity and drug use. While white youth celebrated their so-called "Summer of Love," African Americans were fighting for equality—a battle that continues today with movements like Black Lives Matter.

However, racial tensions have evolved. Some demonstrations today, in their extreme forms, seem to suggest that only certain lives matter, losing the heart of Martin Luther King Jr.'s dream of true equality. Dr. King fought for justice and unity, not division or superiority based on race. Today's movements, in some cases, have strayed from that vision, underscoring how easily rebellion can be twisted into something destructive.

In conclusion, the 1960s were a time of significant societal change, both for good and for bad. The seeds planted in that decade continue to bear fruit today—some of which we see in the moral, social, and spiritual battles of our time. But as God raised up Moses to confront the pharaohs of the past, He is raising up a new generation of leaders, filled with His Spirit, who will stand for truth, confront rebellion, and lead this generation back to Him. Now is the time for us to take our stand and declare that God's way is the only way that leads to life.

MORALE STRATEGY: A CALL FOR A RIGHTEOUS REMNANT

What we desperately need in these last days is a resurgence of morality in our society. As a remnant, those chosen by God to stand firm in faith, it is our mission to re-establish a foundation of righteousness. The key to advancing the Kingdom of God lies in teaching His people to think less about themselves and more about the generation at stake. We must recognize that our religious liberties are tied to the success and influence we have within the culture. Jesus never called us to isolate ourselves but to be set apart, living as a light in a dark world, so that those who are lost might come to know the hope of Jesus Christ.

In today's society, we witness a drastic decline in moral values. What happened to respecting our elders, honoring those in authority, and living lives of integrity? A culture of disrespect and a victim mentality have driven society to its current moral decay. The privilege we have in this nation—the freedom to worship—is something many other countries do not share. In places where the gospel is restricted,

Christians risk their lives to worship and proclaim their faith. We cannot take our freedoms for granted, nor can we let our society continue down this path of destruction without doing something to bring change.

Hatred cannot and will not eradicate hatred. Only love can conquer all. Instead of blaming others, our past, or our race for the state of our generation, we need to take responsibility for being the change agents God has called us to be. Consider the example of Martin Luther King Jr. Raised in a middle-class household, he recognized the injustice of how people were being treated and made the selfless decision to take a stand. Despite the challenges, he pressed forward, tirelessly working and speaking out, trusting God to bring about change. His work changed the course of history, but the full extent of his dream has yet to be realized. That dream now rests in our hands as we continue to fight for equality, justice, and righteousness among all people.

THE CALL TO THE MILLENNIAL, GEN Z, GEN X, GEN ALPHA GENERATION

This generation makes up one-third of the U.S. population. Sadly, a growing number of them identify as "Nones," those who claim no religious affiliation. Many of them, especially through movements like the "Reason Rally" in Washington, D.C., are calling for an America that leaves Christianity behind. They believe it's time to stop using God's Word as a moral guide and replace it with human reasoning alone. But in Isaiah 1:18, God calls us to reason together with Him—acknowledging our sins so He can cleanse and restore us. The problem with the "Nones" and similar movements is that they are trying to reason without God, which leads only to destruction.

"There is a way that seems right to a man, but its end is the way of death."
(Proverbs 14:12)

This is why we see the moral decline of this generation. They have turned their backs on God and are following their own misguided understanding. As a result, many are burdened with financial debt, stress disorders, and broken relationships. The belief that marriage will soon become obsolete is becoming increasingly prevalent, and the emphasis is now on individualism and materialism, rather than on the moral and spiritual values that once upheld our society. In short, they are reasoning without the Creator, which is leading them down a path of destruction.

THE URGENT NEED FOR A REVIVAL IN OUR COLLEGES

The same moral erosion that started in the '60s is now deeply ingrained in our educational institutions. Colleges, which were once pillars of biblical truth, are now breeding grounds for unbiblical ideologies. In 2024, we witnessed widespread protests from college students defending liberal and unbiblical worldviews. This "culture war" on college campuses has intensified, as Satan uses these institutions to indoctrinate young minds and steer them away from God's truth.

But we must not lose hope. There are pockets of revival already taking place in some colleges, where students are boldly declaring their faith in Jesus Christ. We need more of this! We need to pray for our young people and support them as they take their stand in government, healthcare, education, and every other sphere of influence. The enemy's strongholds on these campuses will not last because God is raising up a generation of believers who will turn this nation upside down for His glory.

A CHALLENGE TO BELIEVE IN TRANSFORMATION

The time has come for the people of God to rise up, to restore the moral foundations of our society, and to bring back the standard of righteousness. As we look at the brokenness around us, it can seem overwhelming. But transformation begins with one person who believes in the power of God to change lives. We cannot look at the world through natural eyes; we must see it through the eyes of faith. Jesus said that with God, all things are possible. Even in the face of cultural chaos, we can be agents of change if we commit ourselves to the work of the Gospel.

The journey toward a righteous generation begins with a single step. You and I are called to be that step—to be the remnant that refuses to bow to the pressures of this world. We must raise a new standard, one that points people back to God and shows them the way of life. Through our obedience, we will see transformation in our communities, our schools, our governments, and our world. Let us be bold in our faith, unwavering in our commitment, and relentless in our pursuit of God's will. Together, we will reclaim this generation for Christ.

THE CHALLENGE
#BE AN ONLINE MISSIONARY FOR JESUS

> *He created all the people of the world from one man, Adam, and scattered the nations across the face of the earth. He decided beforehand which should rise and fall, and when. He determined their boundaries. "His purpose in all of this is that they should seek after God, and perhaps feel their way toward him and find him—though he is not far from any one of us."*
> ACTS 17:26–27 ESV

We all have a desire to go out into the world and spread the Good News of Jesus Christ, but often obstacles stand in our way. Whether it's time, travel, or resources, it can seem difficult to fulfill this mission. However, here's the great news: we don't have to get on a plane or travel thousands of miles to share the Gospel. We live in an incredible time where technology, particularly the Internet, provides us with a powerful platform to reach the world for Christ from wherever we are.

While the Internet has been used for ungodly purposes—whether it be sex trafficking, pornography, or other harmful activities—God can use what the enemy meant for evil and turn it for good. We can be a light in the darkness. We can transform the Internet into a tool to spread hope, love, and the message of salvation.

Right now, a digital revival is taking place, and you can be part of it. One way to make an impact is by becoming an online missionary with organizations like Global Media Outreach. From the comfort of your home, you can share the Gospel with people around the world who are seeking the truth. Simply

visit www.globalmediaoutreach.com to sign up and start making a difference.

As you read this, statistics show that an estimated 174,000 people are being drawn to Christ every day. This includes 34,000 South Americans, 30,000 Chinese, 25,000 Africans, and over 16,000 Muslims who are encountering Jesus for the first time. You can play a role in leading more people to salvation by simply sharing your testimony and the message of hope online.

I have experienced this firsthand. One day, while scrolling through Facebook, I reconnected with a friend I hadn't spoken to in over five years. He reached out to ask how I was doing, and I shared my testimony of how God had radically transformed my life during that time. This opened the door for me to minister to him and offer hope in his struggle. He confided in me that despite serving in the Marines, he was battling depression because he hadn't yet discovered God's purpose for his life. Thanks to the Internet, I was able to share the hope of Christ with him, and you can do the same.

You don't need to be a seasoned evangelist or travel far. You can simply type away on your keyboard, share your story, and let Jesus do the rest. The world is waiting for the message of hope that only you can share. Will you accept the challenge? #BeAnAdvocateForJesus.

CHAPTER 6
THE COST OF THE ANOINTING

For the love of money is a root of all kinds of evil. Some people, eager for money, have wandered from the faith and pierced themselves with many grieves.
1 TIMOTHY 6:10 ESV

I hope I shall always possess firmness and virtue enough to maintain what I consider the most enviable of all titles, the character of an honest man.
GEORGE WASHINGTON

In our generation, there's been a dangerous shift in the way we view success. The allure of big stages, large followings, flashy lights, and the showy displays of material wealth have caused many to sell out their anointing. Some have even wandered from the faith in their pursuit of worldly validation, driven by the desire to "make it to the top." But what happens when we trade the eternal for the temporary, the sacred for the superficial?

In Judges chapter 2, God tested the faith of His children through the presence of the Hivites. This group, originating from Canaan's fourth son, embodied a lifestyle that promoted indulgence and selfishness. Their culture was saturated with phrases like "If it feels good, do it," "Don't worry about what others think," and "Look out for number one." Their very name in Hebrew—*Chivim*—means "wicked." They were the same Gibeonites who deceived Joshua into making a peace treaty. In the same way, the enemy today lures us with the wickedness of fleshly desires, trying to pull us away from our calling.

But God is calling this generation to freshen up their anointing, to protect it, and not sell it for the fleeting pleasures of the flesh. The anointing—God's precious empowerment—costs far more than anything this world can offer. It is time to realize that what God has placed on us is worth infinitely more than the temporary thrills and material gains that the world promotes.

THE INTELLIGENCE STRATEGY

If the Israelites had used a strategy of wisdom and discernment as they journeyed through different cultures on their way to the Promised Land, they would have picked up on the ungodly lifestyles of those around them. This same strategy applies to us today. Our goal shouldn't solely be to overcome the lost culture surrounding us, but to understand it. If we take the time to truly understand the mindset of this generation—their desires, their fears, their struggles—then we'll know how to speak directly to the void in their souls.

By engaging with people where they are, listening to their stories, and discerning the root causes of their beliefs and behaviors, we can effectively minister to them. Understanding the culture doesn't mean compromising with it; it means strategically positioning ourselves to bring the truth of God's Word into their hearts and minds in a way that resonates. Jesus himself moved with wisdom and love, engaging people from all walks of life with compassion and truth.

God is raising a generation that will not only resist the temptations of this world but also learn how to navigate its challenges with grace, wisdom, and an unwavering commitment to the anointing. This is the intelligence strategy we need in these last days—understanding the hearts of the lost, so that we can point them to the One who can save them.

Are we willing to pay the cost to keep our anointing? Are we ready to rise and use the wisdom of God to reach a world that is desperately in need of hope? The time is now.

> *For to us a Child shall be born, to us a Son shall be given;*
> *And the government shall be upon His shoulder,*
> *And His name shall be called Wonderful Counselor, Mighty God,*
> *Everlasting Father, Prince of Peace.*
> *There shall be no end to the increase of His government and of peace,*
> *[He shall rule] on the throne of David and over his kingdom,*
> *To establish it and to uphold it with justice and righteousness*
> *From that time forward and forevermore*
> *The zeal of the Lord of hosts will accomplish this.*
> ISAIAH 9:6–7 AMP

ACTIVATE THE ANOINTING

We often view Isaiah 9:6 as a heartwarming verse to read during the Christmas season, but its significance goes far beyond that. Isaiah delivered this prophecy during one of the darkest times for God's people—when sin and idolatry were widespread, and the government opposed those who followed God. The situation is not unlike what we see today, where Christians face persecution worldwide. In some places, the persecution is physical; in others, especially in the West, it's mental and verbal. Every day, I encounter people who struggle with their identity, masking their pain with rebellion against God's principles.

Isaiah, too, witnessed immorality, wickedness, and lawlessness in his time, yet he boldly proclaimed that a child would be born—a child who would carry the weight of a government unlike any other. This was no ordinary child; Isaiah said that the government would rest upon His shoulders, and His name would be called Wonderful Counselor, Mighty God, Everlasting Father, and Prince of Peace. He also declared that the increase of His government would have no end, and it would be established by the zeal of the Lord. This is a profound relief for us today because sometimes we think it's up to us to establish

God's kingdom. But it's the zeal of the Lord that will accomplish it—God invites us to be part of it, but He will bring it to pass.

When Isaiah spoke these words, the people of Israel were under judgment due to their sin and rebellion, similar to the way our generation often refuses to acknowledge God. The Northern Kingdom, despite severe warnings and suffering, proudly claimed to be the master of its destiny. This is the same attitude we see today, where people believe they control their own fate, not realizing that in reality, they are either following God's path or the enemy's. There is no neutral ground. Just like in Isaiah's time, corrupt leaders continue to pass laws that stand against God's principles, and divine judgment is inevitable. Isaiah's refrain, "Yet for all this, His anger is not turned away, His hand is still upraised," illustrates how persistent God's judgment can be when a nation continues to rebel against Him.

"The prophetic voice of our generation has been silenced, but now it's time to speak up."

Isaiah's words remind us of the power of a prophetic voice, both in his time and ours. People don't need to be told what they're doing wrong—they already know. What they need is hope, purpose, and a reason to strive for something greater than themselves. Today, as then, we are called to speak the truth that brings life. Isaiah's declaration of the coming Messiah shifted people's perspectives, filling them with hope in the midst of despair. We, too, must proclaim that same hope in Jesus Christ, the Son of God, who came to establish a kingdom not of this world.

Isaiah gave Jesus four titles: Wonderful Counselor, Mighty God, Everlasting Father, and Prince of Peace. Each of these names spoke directly to the needs of the people in Isaiah's time, just as they speak to our needs today. The people needed guidance and counsel; we, too, need God's wisdom in our lives, our families, and our society. They needed a mighty God to bring deliverance; we need His power today to heal, restore, and break the chains of oppression in this generation. They needed the love and correction of a father; we need to embrace God as our heavenly Father who cares deeply for us. And lastly, the people needed peace in the midst of their captivity, just as we need the Prince of Peace in our world, torn by violence, terror, and unrest.

Imagine how those in Isaiah's day felt when they heard his prophetic words—how their outlook changed as they grasped onto the promise of a coming Savior. In the same way, when we embrace the hope of Christ, our perspective changes, and we begin to walk in purpose. Jesus Christ is our hope, and hope never disappoints.

Today, as prophetic voices, we are called to inject that same hope into our generation. We need to address the root cause of the issues we face, not just the symptoms. We've tried to treat the effects of sin—depression, immorality, and rebellion—without addressing the deeper sickness of our sinful nature. Our task is to call out the greatness that God has placed within this generation and help people see that they are not defined by their past or by the lies of others.

I've met many gifted people who should be thriving, but they are weighed down by the words of those who raised them and the toxic environments they grew up in. Their minds are filled with negativity, and they no longer see their potential. But we cannot live by the words of others; we must live by the words of Christ. I choose to live for an audience of One—Jesus Christ—and speak life over myself based on His truth, not on the opinions of others.

This generation is the most gifted but also the most distracted. The anointing on our lives is too precious to be sold for worldly desires. We are called to be set apart, not for our glory but for the glory of God. Let's rise to the challenge, reclaim the prophetic voice, and lead this generation toward the hope, healing, and peace that only Jesus Christ can provide.

So we are ambassadors for Christ, as though God were making His appeal through us; we [as Christ's representatives] plead with you on behalf of Christ to be reconciled to God.
2 CORINTHIANS 5:20 AMP

In 2 Corinthians 5:20, we are reminded that we are *ambassadors for Christ*, as if God Himself were making His appeal through us. We are Christ's representatives, pleading on His behalf for people to be reconciled to God. This powerful verse points out that we are not just bystanders in God's plan, but active agents in the Kingdom of God.

Isaiah 9:6 says, "The government will rest upon His shoulder." As the body of Christ (1 Corinthians 12:27), we are part of this responsibility, with Jesus as the head and we, the Church, being His body. Just as shoulders carry weight, the responsibility to advance the Kingdom and establish the government of God rests upon us. It is through the gifts He has given us that we contribute to this mission, impacting our communities, workplaces, and society at large. The world is full of distractions, but we must remain focused on our divine assignment.

Consider this: even in an embassy, whether you're a janitor or an ambassador, you still represent your nation. In the same way, no matter our role in the body of Christ, we all carry the weight of God's government upon our shoulders. We are His representatives here on Earth. Whether you see yourself as a "pinky" or an essential part of the body, you are valuable, and God has assigned you a purpose.

Being saved was just the beginning—now, you have a mission to fulfill. And the truth is, none of us can succeed in our mission alone. The body of Christ must function together, and we all need one another to fully carry out God's plans. You may wonder how you can complete your assignment in a world that seems impossible to change. But what is impossible for the natural man is completely possible for the spiritual man through God's power.

1 John 2:20 tells us, *"But you have an anointing from the Holy One."* This means that every believer is equipped and empowered by God's Spirit to carry out their calling. This anointing is not reserved for pastors or highly spiritual individuals; it is for everyone who follows Christ. The anointing is the supernatural empowerment of God that gives you strength and direction to accomplish your mission.

In today's society, this anointing is critical. It is what enables you to navigate life's complexities with wisdom and grace. The anointing will guide you in your career choices, your relationships, your family life, and even how you engage with the racial and societal tensions of our day. It is the anointing that teaches you how to love God deeply and live with purpose beyond attending church on Sundays.

The anointing is not just a religious concept—it is practical and applicable to every area of life. It can help you bring healing to broken relationships, provide clarity in moments of confusion, and give you the courage to stand for righteousness in a world that celebrates sin. Whether you are facing a personal trial, societal challenges, or uncertainty about the future, the anointing of God will equip you to thrive and succeed.

Isaiah 61:1–2 emphasizes the role of the anointing: *"The Spirit of the Lord God is upon me, because the Lord has anointed me to bring good news to the humble and afflicted; He has sent me to bind up the brokenhearted, to proclaim release to captives and freedom to prisoners."* Jesus didn't receive the anointing so He could sit back; neither did He anoint you for that purpose. The anointing has a mission attached to it—to proclaim the good news, heal the brokenhearted, and bring freedom to those in bondage.

In today's context, this anointing empowers us to reach out to the broken and lost, to heal those afflicted by the trials of life, and to declare hope to a generation that feels abandoned and confused. The same Spirit that empowered Jesus to perform miracles, to love the unlovable, and to stand against injustice is living inside of you. This is the same anointing that teaches you how to live, love, and lead in today's challenging environment.

The anointing is not something to be purchased or earned. It is freely given to every believer through Jesus Christ. It is the divine empowerment you need to live a life of impact. Whether you are raising a family, working in the marketplace, or leading a ministry, the anointing will guide you and enable you to fulfill God's purpose for your life. We must awaken to this anointing and walk in its power, knowing that it is the key to living victoriously in every aspect of life.

"But I have an anointing (I am furnished with what is needed from the Holy One [you have been set apart, specially gifted and prepared by the Holy Spirit], and all of you know [the truth because He teaches us, illuminates our minds, and guards us from error].
1 JOHN 2:20 AMP

An example of how the anointing was used in the Old Testament can be found during the time of Moses, specifically through the use of consecrated olive oil. Exodus 25:6 refers to this: "oil for lighting, balsam for the anointing oil and the fragrant incense." God instructed the Israelites to bring oil so that the lamps in the tabernacle would stay lit from morning till evening. This burning oil symbolized the presence of God and relied on the obedience of the people to keep the light burning. Similarly, the anointing in our lives depends on our obedience to the Lord, not just our talents or abilities.

The anointing is not something we can merely receive without preparation. In the book of Exodus, Moses would anoint the priest before they could enter the Holy of Holies to carry out their duties. The anointing oil served as a means of consecration; symbolizing being set apart for God's service:

"You shall anoint Aaron and his sons, and consecrate them, that they may serve as priests to Me. You shall say to the Israelites, 'This shall be a holy and sacred anointing oil, to Me [alone] throughout your generations.'"
Exodus 30:30–31 (AMP)

In the same way, we cannot awaken the anointing inside of us without consecration. To consecrate ourselves means to separate from worldly desires and align with God's purpose. It's not about isolating ourselves physically but about living in such a way that we reflect Jesus in everything we do. We can't water down the gospel to fit into the world—we must stand firm in our faith, even when faced with opposition. Many people want the anointing but are unwilling to set themselves apart for God's work. To consecrate means dying to our own plans and desires to fulfill God's purpose for us.
The Bible says, *"But you are a chosen generation, a royal priesthood, a holy nation, His own special people, that you may proclaim the praises of Him who*

called you out of darkness into His marvelous light."
—1 Peter 2:9 (ESV)

As believers, we are priests in God's kingdom, and just as the priests in the Old Testament had to be anointed before entering the Holy of Holies, we too must be anointed by God before fulfilling our priestly duties in this world. The anointing is not only for ministry but for living out God's calling in every aspect of our lives.

Before receiving the anointing, there is a process of purification and preparation. In Leviticus 8:6–7, Moses washes Aaron and his sons before they were anointed for their priestly duties. Similarly, in our lives, the first step to receiving the anointing is a clean heart. God told Samuel when choosing David, *"Man looks at the outward appearance, but the Lord looks at the heart."* (1 Samuel 16:7). God looks at the state of our hearts before He can release a greater anointing. If our hearts are filled with anger, unforgiveness, pride, or lukewarmness, it becomes difficult for God to pour out His anointing on us.

David was able to defeat Goliath after being anointed, and in the same way, the anointing will empower you to overcome the giants in your life—whether they are giants of sin, financial struggles, fear, or emotional pain. The anointing gives us the strength and authority to face those challenges and come out victorious.

But before we receive the anointing, we must first be washed clean by the blood of Jesus. This cleansing removes the filth of our past sins and prepares us for the robe of righteousness and a new identity in Christ. As we are purified and set apart for God's work, the anointing will flow in our lives, giving us the power to fulfill the calling God has placed upon us.

PROTECT THE ANOINTING

Once the anointing is activated in your life, it is essential to protect it. In Leviticus 21:10-12, priests who were anointed were instructed not to go near a dead body. The principle behind this is clear: the anointing cannot dwell where there is death or sin. Many of us have not fully activated the anointing because we continue to speak death into our lives through negative words, doubt, and toxic relationships.

I remember a time when I was part of a summer internship where we gave scholarships to unchurched kids, including a foster girl who we believed God would transform. But three weeks into the program, she caused disruption and was resistant to change. Leaders had spoken with her, but she remained rebellious. Then the Lord gave me a dream about her and showed me what to do. When I sat with her, she confessed deep pain, saying she started using drugs at just eleven years old. She had never felt truly loved and was angry at God.

Through love and the anointing, we chose not to push her away like others had, but instead embraced her with God's love. She had been surrounded by "dead" relationships, and it was only through choosing life—through forgiveness and love—that she began to experience freedom. For us to be stewards of God's anointing, we too must choose life, not death. The anointing will guide us through our deserts and valleys. You shall not die, but live! Your best days are ahead.

THE PROCESS FOR RECEIVING THE ANOINTING

The anointing is not produced in "baby Christianity" or in casual faith—it is birthed in the depths of spiritual maturity. The anointing grows in times of spiritual revival, hardship, and pressing, much like olive oil is produced through crushing.

The apostle Paul wrote in 2 Corinthians 4:8-12, *"We are hard pressed on every side, but not crushed... struck down, but not destroyed."* Even Jesus, who was from an olive-growing region, would have understood the process of making olive oil: it is extracted through three presses.

The first press of the olive produces oil for light—just as the Holy Spirit gives us light and discernment. The second press produces oil for healing—by Jesus' stripes, we are healed, and the anointing empowers us to bring healing to others. The third press creates oil for soap—symbolizing how Jesus cleanses us from sin.

When the olive is crushed, it releases oil. Likewise, when Jesus was crushed under the weight of our sin, He became the anointing oil that brings healing and life today. If you feel pressed in life, like the weight of the world is on your shoulders, know that the anointing is about to flow out of you. The more we allow ourselves to be refined and crushed in God's process, the more powerful the anointing will be.

The anointing is:
- The seal of God upon your life.
- The Holy Spirit teaching and working through you.
- The source of healing and provision for you and others.
- Strength in difficult times.
- Wisdom and the life of Christ working within you.

God desires to release this anointing in your life to transform the world around you. Just as Jesus changed the course of history through His obedience, the anointing on your life will allow you to stand firm in God's word despite persecution, and to make a lasting impact.

As for me and my house, we pray to be anointed by God. The world may take away material things, but no one can take the anointing—it is a gift from God Himself. Let that be your prayer too: to seek and protect the anointing for your life and for the sake of those around you.

THE PROPHETIC MESSAGE

God desires to increase the anointing in this generation, just as Jesus used His anointing to bring healing, deliverance, and restoration. Jesus set the captives free, broke the chains of those imprisoned by sin and oppression, and opened the eyes of the blind—both physically and spiritually. In the same way, this twenty-first-century generation desperately needs the anointing of God to see those same results in our world today.

We live in a time where many are overwhelmed by financial struggles, chronic illnesses, anxiety, depression, and a loss of hope. Families are broken, addictions run rampant, and countless people are blinded by a culture that leads them further away from God's truth. But through the power of God's anointing, His ambassadors—those of us who follow Christ—are called to bring freedom, healing, and restoration to a world in need.

This generation will rise in the anointing to break the chains of addiction, depression, and fear. They will bring light to those walking in darkness, unveiling the truth of God's love and power to those who are lost. Through God's anointing, we are called to be His hands and feet, bringing transformation to lives, families, and communities. Just as Jesus proclaimed liberty to the captives, we are called to continue His mission, empowered by His Spirit, to see lives restored and hearts healed.

This is the prophetic call for today: to be the vessels through which God's anointing flows, bringing deliverance, healing, and the hope of salvation to all who seek Him.

THE CHALLENGE
#TEST YOUR FAITH

So too, faith, if it does not have works [to back it up], is by itself dead [inoperative and ineffective].
JAMES 2:17 AMP

I want to invite you to take part in a challenge that I believe will reignite and strengthen your faith. Are you feeling spiritually stagnant? Do you feel like you haven't grown in your walk with God? Is your faith no longer being actively relied upon in your daily life? That's a dangerous place to remain.

God calls us to remember where we once were and to return to our first love with Him. Like the church in Revelation, some of us were once strong in faith but have grown complacent. It's time to reignite that fire.

Testing your faith requires stepping into situations where you must fully rely on it. This could mean going on a mission trip that shifts your perspective or visiting a hospital to pray for the sick, trusting God for healing. It's not about trying to earn God's favor through works; rather, it's about putting your faith into action. Faith isn't just something we talk about or share on social media—it's something that God calls us to live out, even in the most challenging circumstances. Sometimes, the only way to grow in faith is to place yourself in a position where your faith is the only thing you can rely on.

CHAPTER 7
STEWARDS OF GRACE

> *"For this reason, I, Paul, am the prisoner of Christ Jesus on behalf of you Gentiles—assuming that you have heard of the stewardship of God's grace that was entrusted to me for your benefit."*
> EPHESIANS 3:1–2 AMP

> *"Let us with caution indulge the supposition that morality can be maintained without religion. Reason and experience both forbid us to expect that national morality can prevail in exclusion of religious principle."*
> GEORGE WASHINGTON

In Judges 3, the **Jebusites** tested God's people on how to stand firm against immorality, a lesson still relevant for us today as we confront the same challenges in our generation. According to *Charisma Magazine*, divorce rates are alarmingly high—up to 50 percent within the church itself! Homosexuality is pulling in more and more young people. These issues are not just in the secular world but within the very walls of the church, a place where marriage should thrive and where men and women should know their God-given identities. The root of today's rampant sexual immorality is the misunderstanding and misuse of grace. Too often, grace is seen as a license to sin rather than the empowerment to overcome temptation and live a life pleasing to God.

Paul reminds us of the stewardship of God's grace, which empowers us to live righteously to be agents of change in these last days, we must grasp the true nature of grace. Unfortunately, the church has often become a sleeping giant, complacent in the face of cultural decay. In 2 Timothy, Paul speaks directly to this issue, urging Timothy to rekindle his faith:

"For this reason I remind you to fan into flame the gracious gift of God, that inner fire which is in you through the laying on of my hands."
2 TIMOTHY 1:6 AMP

Paul's reminder to Timothy is relevant for us today. Just like Timothy, many of us can become discouraged by the culture we live in, questioning our purpose and wondering if God hears our prayers. We may feel stuck in the valleys of life—whether it be family issues, financial struggles, or spiritual stagnation—but it is in these valleys that our trust in God is built. Billy Graham once said, "It is necessary for a Christian to go through the valley because, at the mountaintop, he will appreciate and take better stewardship the next time he reaches it." The valleys teach us to depend on God alone, to trust His purpose for our lives.

Paul goes on to remind Timothy of something even more profound:

"He delivered us and saved us and called us with a holy calling, not because of our works or personal merit but because of His own purpose and grace which was granted to us in Christ Jesus before the world began."
2 TIMOTHY 1:9 AMP

Paul's message is simple: you have been set apart for a life of purpose. This is not something you earned, but something given to you by God's grace. Every believer has two defining moments in their life: the day they are born, and the day they discover *why* they were born. The root of much of today's confusion and chaos stems from this: people, including Christians, do not understand their purpose in Christ. We have world-changers operating out of place, just like cars being used as furniture instead of vehicles for transportation.

This is why our world is chaotic—because people are not living in their God-given design. We are witnessing a culture where liberal and secular ideologies dominate the government, while the children of

God sit by passively, not stepping into their rightful role to influence culture for the kingdom of God.

Paul articulates it beautifully:

> *"My task is to bring out in the open and make plain what God, who created all this in the first place, has been doing in secret and behind the scenes all along. Through followers of Jesus like yourselves, this extraordinary plan of God is becoming known."*
> EPHESIANS 3:8–10 MSG

Our role in this generation is to reveal the mystery of God, hidden for so long, but now made known through Jesus and His church. The ultimate question for each of us is not about what we've *done* for God, but rather, *who* we've become for Him. Did we live our lives as a full expression of His character, love, and grace? Did we truly know Jesus as our Father, or did we simply work for Him without ever knowing Him deeply?

We are living in perilous times: children turning against their parents, parents abandoning their responsibilities, sex and drugs rampant, wars and persecution increasing, and Christians being beheaded for their faith. The world is spiraling downward, yet the church—this sleeping giant—remains passive. We cannot afford to be silent or stagnant any longer. Many believers are caught in a cycle of being saved one week, then falling back into despair the next. This cycle continues because we lack a deep understanding of what Jesus accomplished for us on the cross.

The answer is simple: *we need a fresh understanding of grace*. Not grace as an excuse, but as an empowerment to live holy, set-apart lives that reflect the kingdom of God. Only then will we be able to impact this generation for Christ.

The book of Ephesians provides one of the clearest explanations of the ministry of reconciliation. Written by the Apostle Paul while imprisoned, it reveals the mystery of God's intention to form a body—His church—that would express the fullness of Christ on earth. This wasn't just a message for the church in Ephesus; it's a message for the entire body of Christ. God's plan was to reconcile Jews and Gentiles, uniting all people in His love and grace.

"To the praise of His glorious grace, which He has freely given us in the One He loves. In Him we have redemption through His blood, the forgiveness of sins, in accordance with the riches of God's grace."
EPHESIANS 1:6–7 AMP

This was God's intention: to equip and mature His people so they could extend Christ's victory over evil on earth. The same issues we see today—disunity, confusion, and compromise—were happening back then. Paul was urging believers to grasp the completed work of Christ on the cross, a work that was sufficient to reconcile generations and create one unified people to worship God in spirit and in truth. Jesus' mission on earth was to bring together diverse groups and generations, to form His bride—the church.

Jesus ministered to both Jews and Gentiles, demonstrating the heart of the Father. Ever since the fall in Genesis 3:6, generations have been at odds with one another, as seen in Cain and Abel or Isaac and Ishmael. Jesus came to break these divides and unite us in His love. He came for those who are lost, not for those who think they're already righteous. His heart was to reconcile broken generations, and it should be our mission as well—to bring together those separated by sin and culture under the banner of His love.

LAW VS. GRACE

Today, many believers find themselves trapped in a cycle of sin, feeling powerless to break free. John 1:14 says that Jesus came full of grace and truth, but many are living as if grace is only a vague concept, unsure of how to apply it to their lives. They've been lied to by the enemy, thinking they will never escape certain sins—whether it's immorality, lying, or addiction. But the truth is, grace is not just forgiveness, it is the *empowerment* to overcome sin.

Before we discuss how to live as an empowered church, we need to address the foundation of that empowerment: grace. Too many Christians feel they are not "good enough" or "worthy enough" to walk in the freedom Christ purchased for them.

"I can't be perfect on my own—I need your grace."

One of Satan's most effective strategies is to either tempt us with worldly things or to convince us that we have to earn our salvation. This can be a deadly trap. I once struggled with this myself. I would feel like a failure if I missed a prayer time or fell short in other areas, and I'd strive to make up for it with works—praying longer, trying harder. But one day, the Lord spoke to me, saying, "Stop condemning yourself. You're here praying on a Friday night when you used to be in a club. Quit believing the lie that you are worthless." In that moment, I repented of my efforts to *earn* my salvation and finally embraced God's grace.

"For it is by grace you have been saved, through faith—and this is not from yourselves, it is the gift of God."
EPHESIANS 2:8 NIV

At that moment, I encountered the true meaning of grace. Until we encounter grace, we remain bound by the law, trying to please God through works. The law, which came through Moses, was designed to show us our sin. But the law has no power to save; it only exposes our shortcomings. Living under the law makes us captives, always striving but never measuring up.

GRACE VS. LICENSE TO SIN

While many struggle under the weight of legalism, others have misunderstood grace entirely, using it as a license to sin. They live without the fear of God, believing that grace covers everything, so they continue in their sinful ways without seeking transformation. But grace was never meant to be an excuse for sin; it was meant to *empower* us to live righteously.

Paul reminds us of this in Romans 7:4, saying that we have been put to death in relation to the law through Christ's crucified body so that we can belong to Him and bear fruit for God.

"Therefore, my brothers and sisters, you also were put to death in relation to the law through the body of Christ, that you may belong to another—to Him who was raised from the dead—in order that we might bear fruit for God."
ROMANS 7:4 ESV

Through Jesus' sacrifice, we have been set free from the curse of the law. Grace doesn't just forgive us; it *transforms* us. It empowers us to crucify our sinful nature and its desires so that we can live in freedom and bear fruit for God's kingdom.

THE COST OF GRACE

Grace is not cheap; it came at the highest price—the life of Jesus Christ. Grace should never be taken lightly or misused. It cost more than we could ever repay, and it calls us to live lives of holiness and purpose.

"And those who belong to Christ Jesus have crucified the flesh with its passions and desires."
GALATIANS 5:24 ESV

True grace empowers us to live above sin, to crucify our sinful desires, and to walk in the freedom Christ purchased for us. Grace doesn't just offer us forgiveness, it gives us the strength to overcome the very things that once held us captive. This is the power of grace, and it is the message we must carry to a broken world. Through grace, we are not only reconciled to God, but we are also equipped to extend that reconciliation to others, living as ambassadors of Christ in every area of life.

THE LAW DEMANDS BUT GRACE SUPPLIES

The law demands that we perform, but grace supplies what we need to fulfill God's desires. Under the law, we are required to praise and sacrifice, but grace allows us to offer praise from a heart filled with thanksgiving. The law demands that we keep all 613 commandments, and if we fail at one, we are guilty of all. But grace gives us the strength to live a life that pleases God, not out of obligation, but out of love. The law leaves us with feelings of condemnation and guilt, but grace gives us freedom, a clear conscience, and the power to move forward. The law demands that we work to earn salvation, but grace empowers us to fulfill our calling through the finished work of Christ.

"We have also obtained access through Him by faith into this grace in which we stand, and we rejoice in the hope of the glory of God."
ROMANS 5:2 ESV

Grace is a gift—a state of favor that we stand in, not because of anything we have done, but because of what Christ has done for us. It is by grace that we are no longer slaves to sin but are now free in Christ. We pass from death to life, from sin to righteousness, and we are no longer captives, but free to walk in victory.

True grace cannot be fully understood until we shift from an "Egypt" mentality—a mindset of slavery and bondage—to a kingdom mentality of freedom in Christ. The Israelites struggled to grasp this. Even after being freed from Egypt, they often longed to go back, because they still saw God through the lens of Pharaoh, a harsh taskmaster. They didn't fully see God as a loving Father who cared for them. This is why God had them camp in the wilderness—to show them His kindness and provision. Even in their rebellion, He cared for them, ensuring their clothes and sandals did not wear out for 40 years.

"I led you 40 years in the wilderness; your clothes and the sandals on your feet did not wear out."
DEUTERONOMY 29:5 ESV

This is a perfect picture of grace. Despite their constant rebellion, God's provision never ceased. This same grace is available to us today through Jesus Christ.

GRACE THROUGH JESUS

"Since by the one man's trespass, death reigned through that one man, how much more will those who receive the overflow of grace and the gift of righteousness reign in life through the one man, Jesus Christ."
ROMANS 5:17 ESV

Through Adam's sin, death reigned. But through Jesus, grace and righteousness overflow to those who believe. Grace, in its essence, means kindness, favor, and divine enablement. Grace empowers us to live righteously, keeps us from falling into sin, gives us favor with God, and grants us access to everything we need in Him. It is not earned but freely given, and it is the foundation upon which our relationship with God stands.

The new covenant, which we are under, replaces the old covenant of the law. This covenant is not about external rules but about internal transformation. God writes His laws on our hearts, and we live by the Spirit, empowered by grace.

"Behold, the days will come, says the Lord, when I will make a new covenant with the house of Israel and with the house of Judah… For this is the covenant that I will make with the house of Israel after those days, says the Lord: I will imprint my laws upon their minds, and engrave them upon their hearts. And I will be their God, and they shall be my people."
HEBREWS 8:8–13 AMP

Grace is not just an idea; it is a person—Jesus Christ. Grace is what sets us free from the bondage of sin and the demands of the law. It empowers us to live in freedom, not striving to earn God's favor but resting in the favor we have already received through Jesus.

THE ROLE OF GRACE IN OUR LIVES

Grace is our new identity. It allows us to stand in God's presence without fear, knowing that we are fully accepted because of Christ. It is through grace that we receive all that God has for us—freedom, healing, provision, and purpose. Grace doesn't excuse sin, but it empowers us to overcome it.

"Even when we were dead in trespasses, He made us alive together with Christ—by grace you have been saved."
EPHESIANS 2:5 ESV

When we approach God, we don't come based on our own merits or the good things we've done. We come because Jesus paid the price, and through His grace, we are accepted.

STEWARDS OF GRACE

The Apostle Paul referred to himself as a "steward of grace." This means that, just as Paul carried the message of grace to others, we too are called to be stewards of this gift. Grace is not just for us to receive; it's for us to give.

"Yet grace was given to each one of us in proportion to the measure of Christ's gift."
EPHESIANS 4:7 AMP

We are stewards of God's grace, called to dispense it to those around us. Imagine encountering someone who is struggling with addiction, homelessness, or shame. Instead of judging them, we offer grace. We can say, "I find no fault in you," just as Christ says to us. This grace transforms lives. It's not about condemning people for their sin, but about showing them the love of God that leads to repentance. When we extend grace, we reflect the heart of Jesus, and that grace has the power to change a generation.

This is how the early church spread the gospel across the world—they understood the grace that had been poured out on them, and they were compelled to share it with others. Today, as stewards of grace, we are called to do the same. We are the tools God uses to spread His grace across the earth, changing lives and transforming hearts.

Grace is the key to revival. It empowers us to live as witnesses of the cross, to exercise the authority of the believer, and to show the world the love and mercy of God. This generation will change when we live as stewards of grace, extending it to those who need it most.

MINISTERS OF GRACE

You are called to be a minister of grace to this generation, and you may wonder, "How can I do that?" One of the most powerful ways to minister grace is by how you live your life. Actions often speak louder than words. Let everyone you encounter feel that they are deeply loved. Grace, in its simplest form, can be described as God's overwhelming desire to treat you as though you have never sinned. When we interact with others, we should look for the best in them, not the worst, and speak life into their situations.

One way I personally demonstrate grace is by working with foster children. Many of them have been told their whole lives that they'll never amount to anything, that they're destined to repeat the mistakes of their parents, or that their future holds nothing but pain. Whenever I get the chance, I make it a point to speak positive words over their lives, showing them that their future is bright and full of potential. This, I believe, is a way to be a true steward of grace—by letting people, especially the next generation, know that their story isn't over. They can rise above their circumstances and become a godly remnant that loves Jesus passionately.

One of the greatest examples of grace in action is when Jesus was confronted by the Pharisees who dragged a woman caught in adultery before Him. According to the Law, she deserved to be stoned to death for her sin. They asked Jesus what should be done, expecting Him to confirm her punishment. Instead, He quietly bent down, wrote in the sand, and then said, "Let the one who has never sinned throw the first stone." One by one, the accusers dropped their stones and left, convicted by their own need for grace.

In that moment, Jesus demonstrated that grace should be extended to others, just as it has been given to us. If we are to be the full expression of God's love and grace in this generation, we must respond to people in the same way—choosing grace over judgment, showing compassion instead of condemnation. Through this, we can reflect God's heart and bring healing to those around us.

THE WORD IS ALIVE

God's Word is alive, powerful, and sharp, like a surgeon's scalpel. It cuts through every doubt, defense, and pretense, laying us bare so that we may listen, obey, and be transformed. Nothing can escape its reach. We cannot run from it, nor can we hide from its truth. *"For the word of God is alive and active. Sharper than any double-edged sword, it penetrates even to dividing soul and spirit, joints and marrow; it judges the thoughts and attitudes of the heart. Nothing in all creation is hidden from God's sight. Everything is uncovered and laid bare before the eyes of him to whom we must give account."– Hebrews 4:12-13 (MSG)*

I've witnessed firsthand how God's Word has changed me, and I am confident that this same Word has the power to transform our generation. As you and I live out the message, it won't be long before others start asking about the change they see in us. I remember my own transformation: after surviving a near-fatal car accident, I gave my heart to the Lord, and from that moment on, my life changed radically. I was bound by addictions to alcohol, drugs, lust, and pride. Yet, as soon as I invited Jesus into my heart, it felt like I had received a heart transplant. My old desires were gone. Friends who knew me before were shocked, and they began to ask questions. Within a month of my conversion, I was not only living the message but also sharing it. That's exactly what we need in this generation—a radical display of God's transforming power through our lives.

One of the greatest problems in the church today is the same one Jesus confronted: tradition over relationship. He rebuked the

Pharisees because their man-made traditions made God's Word ineffective. Similarly, many of us are bound by religious traditions that keep us from experiencing the full impact of God's Word. We've become too busy or too distracted to spend time with Him. The tradition says: only the preacher is responsible for sharing the gospel, or you can live holy on Sundays but let your guard down during the week. Traditions like these create a stagnant, powerless faith.

A life governed by tradition leads to a hardened heart. But a relationship with God leads to compassion for the sinner and hatred for the sin. Jesus wants us to move beyond comfortable traditions and pursue Him with total abandonment. The last words of a dying church are, "We've never done it that way before!" Let us refuse to be dying Christians. Instead, let's be transformed and made alive by the power of God's Word, fully prepared to impact our generation for His glory.

MISFIT

"So that you may be blameless and pure, children of God without fault in a warped and crooked generation. Then you will shine among them like stars in the sky."
– Philippians 2:15 (AMP)

There's a misconception in our generation that to be relevant, we must blend in with the world. But Paul is clear: we are called to shine as lights in the darkness, not to become like the world. You don't have to conform to this perverted and crooked generation to be effective. People are longing for authenticity, not a version of Christianity that compromises for the sake of relevance. Jesus didn't seek to exalt Himself, but instead, He humbled Himself to the point of death on a cross. If we want to reflect His light in this generation, we must follow His example—serving others, placing their needs above our own, and living as the message rather than just preaching it.

A "misfit" is someone who doesn't fit into the mold—someone who is different and refuses to compromise in the face of perversion. God will give you the grace to be that light in the midst of darkness. No matter how hard you try to fit in, you were not made to blend in with the world—you were made to stand out, to thrive, and to bring hope.

One of the main reasons for writing this book is to remind us that we can live righteously and holy in this generation. Too often, we let the world's influence creep into our lives, convincing us that we are no different from the culture around us. But today, in Jesus' name, I break that lie. God has given us all the tools and weapons we need to live righteously in the midst of a wicked generation. And this is not the end of our story. We are called to be beacons of light and hope, shining brightly in a dark world. And with God's grace, we will do just that.

THE CHALLENGE
#SHOW GRACE TO SOMEONE
WHO HAS BEEN OUTCAST BY SOCIETY

In this chapter, we've explored what it means to be stewards of grace. Now, I want to challenge you to take that grace and extend it to someone who doesn't know God. This could be through organizing a homeless outreach at your church, or even just going out on your own to make a difference. Every city has a population of homeless people who are in need, and showing them God's grace can have a powerful impact.

I remember every time our church organized a homeless outreach, we prepared a meal and brought it to one of the areas in our city where the homeless gather. What amazed me was how I often felt more blessed by the experience than they did. Seeing the joy on their faces as they received a simple meal and a kind word reminded me of the overwhelming grace God has shown in my own life.

Many times, they would ask, "Why are you doing this?" And I would tell them, "This is God's grace for you. He always gives us more than we deserve."

Don't be afraid to step out and extend grace to others in a tangible way. Whether it's through a simple act of kindness or a larger outreach, you can be a vessel of God's grace in someone's life—just as Christ has been in yours.

CHAPTER 8
MOTHERS OF BREAKTHROUGH: BREAKING GENERATIONAL CHAINS

And Ruth said, urge me not to leave you or to turn back from following you; for where you go I will go, and where you lodge I will lodge. Your people shall be my people and your God my God.
RUTH 1:16 AMP

We ought not to look back unless it is to derive useful lessons from past errors, and for the purpose of profiting by dear bought experience.
GEORGE WASHINGTON

The artist Sarah Walker once said, "Becoming a mother is like discovering the existence of a strange new room in the house where you already live." This description powerfully captures the depth and transformation motherhood brings. A mother plays a critical role in shaping the next generation, serving as the first expression of love that a child experiences upon entering the world. When a woman carries a child, she isn't just living for herself—she becomes a vessel of life, entrusted with a sacred responsibility.

"A mother can turn a curse into a legacy."

Personally, I owe an immeasurable debt to my own mother. Even when everyone else had given up on me, she never wavered. During the darkest days of my life, when I was lost in the world—bound by sin and lawlessness—my mother was on her knees, fervently praying. While I was out partying or engaging in destructive behaviors, she stood in the gap, praying and believing that God would bring me back to Him. Others told her I was hopeless, that I would never change, but she refused to stop pleading with God for my soul.

I was living under a curse, heading toward destruction, but through her relentless prayers and unwavering faith, she helped transform my curse into a legacy of redemption. I believe this type of steadfast, praying mother is needed more than ever in our generation—women who will not be intimidated by the enemy's schemes but will stand firm on God's promises, fighting for their children's destinies.

Today, we live in a culture that promotes the idea of "women's rights" in a way that often prioritizes personal autonomy over the gift of life. While I understand that some women face tragic circumstances like abuse, abortion is not the answer. I've met people whose mothers considered abortion after experiencing abuse, but through God's intervention and the persuasion of loving individuals, those children were given the chance to live—and they have gone on to become mighty warriors for God. Their impact is undeniable, and had their lives been terminated, the world would have missed out on their God-given potential.

Abortion is often framed as a "right," but it's actually a grave sin disguised as a choice. Many women who have undergone abortions suffer long-term emotional scars, but Jesus is the healer. Let's look to Scripture to understand what God says about the value of life and the sanctity of the womb. We cannot ignore the staggering reality: according to the World Health Organization (WHO), 40–50 million abortions occur globally every year, which amounts to about 125,000 abortions per day.

125,000 ABORTIONS PER DAY

In the United States alone, approximately 974,000 abortions were performed in 2014, down from over 1 million in previous years. From 1973 to 2011, nearly 53 million legal abortions took place in the U.S. alone. How can these numbers not break our hearts? But the real question is, how do we change this tragic reality? We need to address the root issue by focusing on restoring the family, starting with mothers who carry the power to break curses and pass on blessings.

THE VALUE OF EVERY LIFE

Many political and social leaders argue that abortion is a woman's right, but I would ask them: "What if your mother had decided to abort you?" The unborn child has no voice, no choice, and yet their right to life is debated as if it were optional. This isn't a political issue; it's a spiritual one. The decision to abort isn't about choice—it's about whether we value life, the life that God has created and entrusted to mothers.

BREAKING GENERATIONAL CURSES

Proverbs 30:11 says, "There is a generation that curses its father and does not bless its mother." Curses, whether spiritual or generational, are real. They are often passed down because of sin. Just as physical traits and health conditions can be inherited from parents, so can spiritual conditions. If a family has a history of certain sins—whether it's promiscuity, addiction, or anger—those curses can continue until they are broken by the power of Jesus.

Jesus himself acknowledged the reality of generational curses. When His disciples asked Him whether a man's blindness was due to his own sin or his parents', Jesus didn't dismiss the question because He understood that spiritual inheritances are real. Curses don't simply vanish when someone accepts Christ; they must be confronted and broken through the authority of Jesus. Mothers today need to recognize the spiritual battle for their children and stand firm in prayer to break these curses and protect their children's destinies.

Exodus 20:5 reminds us: "I, the Lord your God, am a jealous God, punishing the children for the sin of the parents to the third and fourth generation of those who hate me."

This is why it's crucial for mothers and fathers to understand the long-term consequences of their choices—not just for themselves, but for their children and grandchildren. The decisions we make today echo through the generations, either as blessings or curses. But praise be to God, who through Jesus Christ, gives us the power to break these curses and establish blessings.

We see examples throughout Scripture of spirits and curses attacking children, whether it was a demon tormenting a boy in Mark 9:21 or a woman's daughter in Matthew 15:22. The enemy's strategy is clear: he targets the young, those who have great purpose, in an attempt to thwart God's plan. The abortion crisis is just one more manifestation of this spiritual battle. Yet, we know that God has promised to pour out His Spirit in these last days, empowering the next generation to prophesy, see visions, and dream dreams (Joel 2:28).

The enemy knows this, which is why he's trying to destroy this generation before they even enter the world. But mothers, you have the power through Christ to break these curses, protect your children, and raise up a generation that will walk in the light and fulfill God's purposes.

LOT AND HIS WIFE

In Genesis 19, we learn about Lot, Abraham's cousin, who lived in the city of Sodom with his wife and two daughters. The sin in Sodom and Gomorrah had become so overwhelming that God decided to destroy the cities. However, because of Abraham's intercession, God sent angels to warn and rescue Lot and his family before His judgment came upon the land. When the angels arrived, Lot welcomed them into his home. However, the men of the city, consumed with wickedness, surrounded Lot's house and demanded to have relations with the visitors.

Genesis 19:4–7 (AMP) says: "But before they lay down, the men of the city of Sodom, both young and old, all the men from every quarter, surrounded the house. And they called to Lot and said, 'Where are the men who came to you tonight? Bring them out to us, that we may know (be intimate with) them.' And Lot went out to them, shutting the door behind him, and said, 'I beg of you, my brothers, do not behave so wickedly.'"

Seeing the depravity of the city, the angels urged Lot to gather his family and flee immediately. As they left, the angels specifically commanded them not to look back, symbolizing a complete break from the sinful past. Despite the warning, Lot's wife disobeyed, looking back longingly at the life she was leaving behind, and as a result, she was turned into a pillar of salt (Genesis 19:26). Her attachment to her past cost her the future that God had prepared for her.

THE SPIRIT OF FEAR

Lot and his two daughters managed to escape to the mountains, but a spirit of fear began to overwhelm his daughters. They feared the end of their family line, believing that there were no men left to continue their lineage. This fear, much like the fear that plagued their mother, drove them to make a terrible decision. In their desperation, they got their father drunk and committed incest, leading to the birth of Moab and Ben-ammi, the ancestors of the Moabites and Ammonites (Genesis 19:31–38). This passage shows how the same spirit of fear that caused Lot's wife to look back also influenced the actions of her daughters. The curse of fear followed this family, leading them to unthinkable choices.

GENERATIONAL CURSES AND THEIR IMPACT

This story is a powerful example of how generational curses can affect families. Lot was a righteous man, yet his family suffered because of fear and sin. Just like Lot's daughters, many of us today are dealing with generational issues—poverty, broken homes, sickness, addiction—that have been passed down through our bloodlines. The Bible tells us in Romans 5:12 that sin entered the world through one man, and with it came death and suffering.

Leviticus 17:11 (ESV) reminds us: "For the life of the flesh is in the blood." This tells us that just as physical traits are passed down, so too are spiritual and *emotional burdens. If we don't recognize and break these curses, they can continue to affect future generations, as we see in Lot's family.*

Curses manifest in many ways: through poverty, infidelity, addiction, and broken homes. These issues persist because no one has taken the time to identify and break the cycle. Whether in Latino, African American, or Anglo communities, these generational struggles—like fatherless homes, violence, or divorce—are evident. The question is: How do we stop these curses?

TRACE IT, ERASE IT, REPLACE IT

As my spiritual mentor, Mark Vega, taught me: Trace the issue, Erase it through repentance, and Replace it with the truth of God's Word. Exodus 20:5-6 (AMP) says that the iniquities of the fathers are visited upon their children to the third and fourth generations, but God also promises mercy to those who love Him and keep His commandments. The key to breaking generational curses is through repentance and living according to God's Word.

In my own family, I pray to break the curse of unfaithfulness. I declare that my future children will not inherit the sins of their forefathers. We can all do this by recognizing patterns, repenting on behalf of those who came before us, and replacing those curses with the blessings that come through a relationship with Jesus Christ. He has already broken every curse through His sacrifice on the cross, and it is by His blood that we are set free.

"Whom the Son sets free is free indeed" (John 8:36).

RUTH: THE REDEEMER'S LEGACY - BREAKING THE CHAINS OF GENERATIONAL CURSES

In the book of Ruth, we are given a powerful example of how a woman can rise up and break generational curses for her family and future generations. Ruth's story begins with her mother-in-law, Naomi, who was married to Elimelech. Together, they had two sons named Mahlon and Chilion. During a time of famine, they moved from Bethlehem to Moab, where Elimelech eventually died, leaving Naomi with her two sons. These sons married Moabite women, Ruth and Orpah, but tragedy struck again as both sons also passed away. This left Naomi, Ruth, and Orpah as widows in a land with a history of deep spiritual curses.

To understand the significance of this, we must look back at Lot's story. Lot, Abraham's nephew, fled to the mountains of Moab after the destruction of Sodom and Gomorrah. Lot's daughters, driven by fear and desperation, committed a grievous sin by having children with their father. This sin left a lasting curse on their descendants, the Moabites, which carried on through generations. Ruth and Orpah, as Moabites, were part of that cursed lineage.

As we see in the account, Ruth and Orpah lost their husbands and faced a critical decision: remain in Moab or return to Bethlehem with Naomi. Both women had lived under the spiritual weight of their ancestral curses, yet something about Naomi's God had stirred their hearts. Ruth, in particular, was determined to break free. She made a bold decision that would alter the course of her life and her lineage.

When Naomi urged her daughters-in-law to return to their own people, Ruth responded with one of the most powerful declarations in Scripture:

"Don't urge me to leave you or to turn back from you. Where you go, I will go, and where you stay, I will stay. Your people will be my people and your God, my God."
RUTH 1:16 ESV

Ruth refused to return to a cursed existence. She refused to carry the generational sin that had plagued her people. Instead, she chose the God of Israel, a God who could break the curse and redeem her life. Ruth traced the source of her suffering and erased it through faith, repentance, and a firm commitment to follow God. Her decision brought her into the lineage of Jesus Christ, the ultimate Redeemer.

Because of Ruth's obedience and faith, she married Boaz, the kinsman-redeemer, and their descendants include King David, and ultimately, Jesus Christ. Ruth went from being a woman burdened by a curse to being part of the lineage that would bring salvation to the world.

Women of God today, just like Ruth, you have the power to break curses that may have followed your family for generations. There comes a moment when you must draw a line in the sand and declare, "Enough is enough." Through prayer, repentance, and unwavering faith, you can break the chains of past sins and reclaim your family's future in the name of Jesus. Just as Ruth broke free from her past and forged a new legacy, so can you.

We live in a time where some mothers are more focused on material gain than on raising a godly generation. But Ruth's example teaches us that it's not the pursuit of worldly things that will change the future—it's a life surrendered to God, a life of prayer and faith. Ruth changed the trajectory of her family and became a part of the greatest redemptive story ever told.

You too, can be a curse breaker. Pray for your children. Declare God's promises over your family. Be like Ruth—a woman of faith, courage, and obedience. Just as she changed her lineage for eternity, so can you impact your generation and the ones to come. May we see more mothers who, like Ruth, choose God and His righteousness over everything else, paving the way for spiritual revival and blessing in their families.

THE CHALLENGE
#FORGIVE SOMEONE IN YOUR FAMILY WHO HAS HURT YOU

> *Whenever you stand praying, if you have anything against anyone, forgive him [drop the issue, let it go], so that your Father who is in heaven will also forgive you your transgressions and wrongdoings [against Him and others]. "But if you do not forgive, neither will your Father in heaven forgive your transgressions."*
> MARK 11:25–26 AMP

As we conclude the chapter on being a curse breaker, it's important to highlight a critical step in breaking the chains that bind us—forgiveness. In my travels, I've discovered that many people carry curses in their lives simply because they are holding onto unforgiveness, especially toward family members or those close to them. Often, the areas in which they experience struggle are directly related to a past wound—whether from abuse, neglect, or betrayal.

We need to remember that forgiveness isn't just about freeing the other person—it's about freeing ourselves. When we forgive, we release the hold that bitterness, anger, and pain have on our lives. Forgiveness is key to personal healing and breaking spiritual strongholds that hinder us. This generation desperately needs people who are free from these chains in order to bring freedom to others.

In my experience, when praying for individuals struggling under the weight of a curse, the Holy Spirit frequently leads me to encourage them to forgive. The moment they forgive a father who hurt them, a mother who wronged them, or any other person from their past, I can often sense the spiritual release as if literal chains are falling away. Healing begins the moment they let go of the unforgiveness they've been holding onto.

Many in this generation are living lives weighed down by incidents from their childhood—unresolved wounds that have festered over time. The division, bitterness, and grudges we see so often could be erased if we would simply follow the biblical call to forgive one another. It's time to let go of the past, heal from the pain, and forgive, so that God's freedom can flow through us and bring healing to our families, communities, and generation.

CHAPTER 9
RESTORING THE FATHER'S ROLE: HEALING A FATHERLESS GENERATION

On that day I will carry out against Eli everything that I have spoken concerning his house (family), from beginning to end. Now I have told him that I am about to judge his house forever for the sinful behavior, which he knew [was happening], because his sons were bringing a curse on themselves [dishonoring and blaspheming God] and he did not rebuke them.
1 SAMUEL 3:12–13 AMP

The hand of providence has been so conspicuous in all this, that he must be worse than an infidel that lacks faith, and more than a wicked, that has not gratitude enough to acknowledge his obligations.
GEORGE WASHINGTON

In 2016, the National Fatherhood Initiative reported that 24 million children in America—about one in every three—are growing up in homes without their biological fathers. According to the U.S. Census Bureau, this fatherless epidemic is acknowledged by nine out of ten American parents as a national crisis. The effects are staggering: 70 percent of inmates in our prisons come from fatherless homes, and 80 percent of rapists were raised without fathers. These statistics are not confined to men in prison— they extend to those still free. For example, 71 percent of high school dropouts come from homes without a father, and 63 percent of all teen suicides occur in fatherless households. These are just some of the devastating impacts when men fail to take responsibility for their role in the family.

In today's generation, we see too many men who walk away, whether from marriages, relationships, or even brief encounters that result in pregnancy. As Dr. Tony Evans powerfully said, "They are not just walking out on the woman; they are abandoning their divine role as men of God, failing in their duty not only to their homes but to their communities, churches, cities, and ultimately, the world. When a father abandons his home, the ripple effect of that absence impacts everything."

This "fatherless factor" is a contributing element to many of the social crises we face in America today. The effects of fathers walking away—whether physically absent or emotionally disconnected—are felt in every aspect of society. Even those fathers who are present but neglectful still leave wounds.

As Tony Evans points out in his book *Kingdom Man*, taxpayers spend more than $8 billion annually on public assistance programs for high school dropouts, many of whom come from fatherless homes. Dropouts earn an average of $260,000 less over their lifetime, resulting in a national economic loss of over $300 billion in lost taxable revenue. Teen pregnancies cost taxpayers $10 billion annually in public assistance, lost revenue, and healthcare costs. Even more troubling is the fact that the prison population has nearly tripled between 1987 and 2007. Today, we spend over $52 billion a year on prisons.

We are undeniably in a crisis. You don't need to look far to see the effects of absent fathers—you may see it in your own family, among friends, or within your community. Men, who were meant to lead, have fallen into destructive patterns, leaving behind broken homes. The question we must ask is: How do we fix this?

I believe the tools shared throughout this book are essential in guiding us toward restoration, but now I want to get more personal as we begin to break down the family structure, starting with mothers and now turning to fathers. As a foster care worker, I've witnessed firsthand the deep trauma inflicted on children raised without fathers. The emotional scars these children carry are unimaginable. If only those absent fathers knew the lifelong consequences their departure would have on their kids.

SETTING THE HOUSE IN ORDER

This fatherless crisis did not start with the millennial generation; it dates back to biblical times. Consider the story of Eli, the priest, in 1 Samuel. Eli served as the spiritual leader of Israel, but in his later years, he became passive in his role. The Bible says that in those days, "the word of the Lord was rare" (1 Samuel 3:1), which is a reflection of how disconnected Eli had become from the voice of God.

God called Samuel, who served under Eli, to deliver a difficult message: judgment was coming to Eli's household because of his failure to correct the sinful behavior of his sons. They had brought a curse upon themselves by blaspheming God, and Eli, despite knowing this, did not intervene. The Bible says that Eli's sons were stealing the sacrifices meant for the Lord and even sleeping with the women who served at the entrance of the Tent of Meeting.

Eli's passivity in addressing the wrongdoing of his sons is reflective of what we see in many homes today. Too many fathers witness their children making poor decisions and simply issue verbal warnings without taking meaningful action. It's not enough to be passive; we need fathers who will actively correct, guide, and enforce God's will in their homes. Because Eli failed to act, he lost his calling and his sons to sin.

The Bible provides us with a powerful lesson through Eli's story. Fathers are called to actively participate in their children's lives, both spiritually and emotionally. A father's absence, whether through neglect or physical absence, leaves a void that cannot easily be filled. Fathers are meant to be the priests of their homes, but when they abdicate that role, the consequences ripple through the entire family, church, community, and even nation.

One of the critical issues is the imbalance of influence in the home. Many fathers work long hours and spend little time with their children, leaving mothers and other caregivers to provide the majority of the guidance. When fathers are only present for a few hours a day, children learn mostly from the women in their lives. This is not to diminish the role of mothers, but it highlights the need for balance. Fathers must be intentional about investing time with their children, being present at meals, and imparting wisdom and guidance.

In Jewish culture, the family meal was a time for fathers to teach, encourage, and strengthen family bonds. But in many modern homes, family members eat in separate rooms, absorbed in their own distractions. Technology, busyness, and tolerance of lax standards have crept into the family institution, contributing to the breakdown of the home. We must return to the table—to intentional, God-centered family time—if we want to see real change in our homes and communities.

The story of Eli and his sons teaches us that fathers cannot afford to be passive. They must take an active role in guiding and correcting their children. The enemy is serious about destroying families, and we must be equally serious about protecting them. Fathers, take up your calling. Your responsibility is not just to carry the title of "father" but to live out what it means to be a godly example, a leader, and a protector of your family.

THE OUTCOME OF ELI AND HIS SONS: A WARNING FOR FATHERS TODAY

In the battle between the Israelites and the Philistines, the Israelites were not only defeated, but they suffered a tremendous loss—30,000 soldiers fell that day. Worse yet, the Ark of God was taken, and Eli's two sons, Hophni and Phinehas, were killed. When news of this disaster reached Shiloh, Eli, who was anxiously waiting, received the devastating report: Israel was defeated, his sons were dead, and the Ark of God had been captured. The shock was too much for Eli. He fell backward from his seat, broke his neck, and died. This marked the tragic end of a family line that once had great spiritual authority over Israel. Eli had judged Israel for forty years, yet the consequences of his failure as a father were severe (1 Samuel 4:10–18 ESV).

Unfortunately, this is not just a story from ancient times—it's a modern reality. We see similar outcomes in families today, where fathers abandon their roles, either by leaving entirely or by being emotionally absent. Many fathers, whether through neglect or distraction, fail to provide the leadership and spiritual covering their families need. And when fathers abdicate their responsibility, the enemy finds his way into the home, bringing destruction in the form of broken relationships, rebellion, and spiritual apathy. This is not a hypothetical issue but a real-life crisis. We need Kingdom fathers more than ever—men who will step up and exercise their God-given authority in the home.

EXERCISE YOUR AUTHORITY

One of the key reasons we see so many fathers stepping away from their roles is a misconception that God will take care of everything for them. Many men have bought into the religious lie that "God is in control" means they don't have to take action in their homes. But this is a misunderstanding. God gave authority to Adam and Eve to have dominion over the earth, and when Adam failed to follow God's instructions, that authority was forfeited to Satan, who then became the "god of this world." However, through Christ, we have been given the power to reclaim that authority.

Fathers often ask, "Why are my children going astray when I've brought them to church every Sunday? Why am I not seeing the results I've prayed for in my home?" The issue, as Jesus pointed out to the religious leaders of His time, is that tradition and religion can render the Word of God powerless when they are not accompanied by faith. *"Thus you nullify the word of God by your tradition that you have handed down."* *(Mark 7:13)*

When fathers reduce their relationship with God to a set of religious activities instead of a vibrant, living relationship, the Word becomes ineffective in their lives. Fathers, if your faith is only a routine, it won't have the impact you desire on your family. Many men find it easier to trust in their own efforts than to fully rely on God, especially in times of financial or family struggles. But trusting God is essential for exercising the spiritual authority given to us.

Today, fathers spend hours at sporting events, watching games, and engaging in hobbies, but how much time is invested in the spiritual growth of their families? Imagine if the same energy spent on a football game was applied to the things of God—what transformation could take place? We have become so distracted by the temporal that we've forgotten the eternal impact of our roles as fathers. It's time to shift our priorities back to where they belong.

THE CALL TO GUARD AND PROTECT

From the beginning, God placed Adam in the garden and gave him specific instructions to guard and protect it. Adam had a direct revelation from God, and it was his responsibility to exercise authority over the garden. However, when Eve came into the picture, Satan targeted her because she received translated knowledge from Adam, not direct revelation from God. This distinction is important because it reveals why Satan went after Eve—he knew that Adam, with revealed knowledge, would not easily be deceived.

"The Lord God took the man and put him in the Garden of Eden to work it and take care of it." (Genesis 2:15)

When fathers don't have a direct, intimate relationship with God, they rely on second-hand knowledge, leaving their families vulnerable to attack. This is why fathers need to be engaged in their spiritual life and lead their families with revelation, not just routine. The enemy exploited Eve's lack of direct revelation, and Adam, instead of stepping in to protect her and exercise his authority, stood by passively.

The same passive behavior that we saw in Adam and Eli is what we see in many fathers today. They know what's right, but they don't act. Fathers, God has given you the authority to protect and lead your family. Don't let the enemy find an open door through your passivity. When something is wrong in your home, don't ignore it—address it, pray over it, and seek God's guidance on how to bring correction.

A CALL TO ACTION: PUT YOUR HOUSE IN ORDER

To put your house in order, you must first put yourself in order. You cannot lead your family if your own life is in chaos. Start by deepening your relationship with God, repenting where necessary, and seeking His guidance on how to be the father He has called you to be. Your role as a father is not just to provide financially or physically but to be the spiritual leader of your home.

Strengthen your relationship with your wife—pray with her, encourage her, and build her up. She is your partner in raising godly children, not just someone to help manage the home. And with your children, take the time to teach, love, and correct them. Don't just have children—raise them to be followers of Christ who will stand strong in a world that desperately needs godly men and women.

This generation will only change when fathers return to their God-given roles, leading their families in truth, love, and righteousness. Fathers, the time to act is now. Don't wait for another crisis to force your hand. Begin today to put your house in order, and watch how God uses your obedience to bring revival to your family and beyond.

THE CHALLENGE
#BE A MENTOR TO SOMEONE YOUNGER

Train up a child in the way he should go and when he is old he will not depart from it.
PROVERBS 22:6 ESV

Check out the movie *The Forge*, which highlights the importance of mentorship and becoming a man of valor. Since I gave my life to Christ in 2011 and joined Bible college, I've had the privilege of being surrounded by some incredible world changers. During that time, I noticed that many of my friends had never experienced true mentorship—someone who would challenge, counsel, and stand by them during tough times.

If we want to make a lasting impact on this generation, we need to begin with discipleship. Jesus commanded us to make disciples, not just converts. Unfortunately, one of the greatest shortcomings in the church today is the lack of genuine discipleship for the younger generation. This is why many young people turn to gangs or worldly influences—they find more mentorship and brotherhood outside the church than within it.

AZAEL NUÑEZ

CHAPTER 10
CALLED TO DELIVER: THE YOUNG GENERATION'S ROLE IN REVIVAL

Jesus summoned His twelve disciples and gave them authority and power over unclean spirits, to cast them out, and to heal every kind of disease and every kind of sickness.
MATTHEW 10:1 AMP

Let your heart feel for the afflictions and distress of everyone, and let your hand give in proportion to your purse.
GEORGE WASHINGTON

Throughout the Bible, we see God raising young people to become deliverers in their generation. Joseph was a young dreamer, Joshua a young successor, Gideon a young farmer, Samuel a young prophet, David a young shepherd, Jeremiah a young prophet, and even Jesus was a young savior. The disciples themselves were young world changers. These young people had one thing in common: they were called by God to deliver their generation. The question for you today is: Will you rise up to deliver your generation?

"The reason you've been through what you've been through is because you carry deliverance."

There is purpose in the struggles you've faced. You are a carrier of deliverance, and the things you've overcome are now part of your testimony to help others find freedom. If you once struggled with cutting, it's because you are called to help set free those who are bound by the same struggle. If you battled with fear, it's so you can help others break free from fear. If you were caught in addiction or sexual immorality, God can use your story to bring healing and freedom to others. Even if you've led a life free from many of these struggles, you are a witness to a generation looking for examples of godliness.

Always remember, the trials you have overcome are the keys to unlocking someone else's freedom. While it was not God's plan for you to face these hardships, He has turned them into testimonies for His glory, enabling you to bring deliverance to others.

The purpose of this book is to awaken the deliverer inside you—to stir the power of love that sets captives free. Just as Jesus was sent to deliver, He has passed that same mission to us. He has empowered us to cast out unclean spirits and heal every disease and sickness. So why is it that instead of being deliverers, many in this generation are captives of the world?

SOCIAL MEDIA PHENOMENON

Jesus warned us: "On the day of judgment, you will give an account for every idle word you speak."
— Matthew 12:36 (AMP)

If your life's story were captured solely through social media—through your snaps and posts—what would it reveal?

In times past, children were primarily raised by their parents, influenced by the example set before them. Today, many young people are being raised by something else: the internet. Social media, Hollywood, and the music industry have become the mentors for our youth. The values they adopt, the advice they follow, and the examples they imitate often come from these virtual platforms rather than from their families.

Social media is a driving force behind the *"Snapchat generation"*. According to statistics, billions of videos are viewed on Snapchat every day, with a vast majority of users between the ages of 18 and 29. The appeal of the app lies in its temporary nature—posts disappear within 24 hours, leaving no trace, creating an illusion of freedom from consequences.

But the problem is, in that fleeting moment, people often act in ways they wouldn't in person. They believe their actions have no lasting impact, forgetting that while social media might erase their posts, nothing is hidden from God. Imagine standing before God one day and realizing that your words, your actions, and your online persona will all be reviewed—not by your peers, but by the Creator Himself. Jesus said we would give an account for every idle word, every careless action. How much more will we be held accountable for the things we do online?

This generation is driven by a desire for attention: "How many likes did I get?" "How many followers?" "What can I do to get more?" But this pursuit of validation from the world is empty. We were created not for the praises of man but to live in the praise of God.

God is calling you to something greater. You are meant to be a deliverer, not a captive to the world's fleeting desires. The young generation has the power to bring about change—real, lasting change—not through social media likes, but through a life lived for God.

"MORE THAN YOLO: LIVING WITH PURPOSE BEYOND THE MOMENT"

"For this is how God loved the world: He gave His one and only Son, so that everyone who believes in Him will not perish but have eternal life. God sent His Son into the world not to judge the world, but to save the world through Him. There is no judgment against anyone who believes in Him. But anyone who does not believe in Him has already been judged for not believing in God's one and only Son."
— John 3:16–18 (AMP)

In today's culture, "You Only Live Once" (YOLO) has become a mantra. It encourages people to live in the moment and chase temporary thrills as if this life is all that matters. But if we truly only live once, shouldn't we make it count for something more meaningful and eternal? Instead of focusing on things that fade, we should invest in what lasts—our relationship with God and our impact on others.

I've had the privilege of working with young people from all walks of life, from those who are on fire for God to those trapped in destructive lifestyles. One common thread I've noticed is that young people often act like they have it all figured out, avoiding help even when they desperately need it. Many times, they mask their pain with defiance or seek comfort in temporary pleasures. But at some point, the truth of God's love reaches us all, just as it did me.

"For God so loved me that He gave His only Son"—this truth hit me like a wave when I was lost in darkness. It was the love I never knew I needed. The reason so many young people reject God's love is because they've never experienced real, unconditional love. Many are carrying deep wounds from the past, and some have even experienced abuse from people they should have trusted—sometimes even within the church.

Shame is a powerful prison that keeps many young people from accepting God's love. I was molested by someone I trusted as a child, and that pain led me down a dark path. I tried to bury it, convinced I had the right to hurt others because of what was done to me. Like many today, I bought into the lie that living recklessly, hurting others, and chasing fleeting pleasures was justified.

But the truth is, what we go through doesn't disappear like a Snapchat post. Those painful memories don't just vanish; they stay imprinted on our hearts. The world tells us we can erase them by indulging in distractions, but only Jesus can truly heal those wounds and help us forgive ourselves.

Jesus didn't come to shame us for our past; He came to free us from it. I once ministered to a young girl who had been abused and abandoned by her parents. She carried such deep pain that every attempt to help her was met with anger and rejection. But I knew that, like so many young people today, her anger was a mask for the hurt she didn't know how to express. She, like others, was trapped in a YOLO mindset—crying out for help but unsure where to find it.

In another instance, I prayed for a girl who was tormented by voices telling her to end her life. She couldn't even stay in the church service because the voices in her mind were louder than the worship music. But that night, we prayed over her as a group, and by the power of Jesus' name, those voices were silenced. She was delivered from the torment that had held her captive.

If you are struggling, whether you're young or old, know this: You were created for more than just the moment. God loves you so much that He sent His Son, not just to give you a temporary escape, but to give you eternal freedom. Whatever voices of condemnation you're hearing, command them to leave in the name of Jesus. Break every agreement with lies and step into the light of God's truth.

INSTA STORIES: DON'T DISQUALIFY YOURSELF—GOD HAS MORE IN STORE

"The angel of the Lord appeared to him and said, 'Mighty hero, the Lord is with you!'"
— Judges 6:12 NLT

Have you ever asked yourself, "Why does God keep pursuing me? I'm nobody. I don't have a purpose. My life feels like a failure. My family is a mess. I'm being bullied, and I don't see a reason to keep going." If you've had these thoughts, you're not alone—Gideon felt exactly the same. He lived in difficult times, oppressed by enemies who took everything from him. He felt helpless and unworthy, but one day, God sent an angel with a message that would change his life:

"Then the angel of the Lord came and sat beneath the great tree at Ophrah, which belonged to Joash of the clan of Abiezer. Gideon, son of Joash, was threshing wheat at the bottom of a winepress to hide the grain from the Midianites. The angel of the Lord appeared to him and said, 'Mighty hero, the

Lord is with you!'
'Sir,' Gideon replied, 'if the Lord is with us, why has all this happened to us? And where are all the miracles our ancestors told us about? Didn't they say, "The Lord brought us up out of Egypt"? But now the Lord has abandoned us and handed us over to the Midianites.'
Then the Lord turned to him and said, 'Go with the strength you have, and rescue Israel from the Midianites. I am sending you!'
'But Lord,' Gideon replied, 'how can I rescue Israel? My clan is the weakest in the whole tribe of Manasseh, and I am the least in my entire family!'
The Lord said to him, 'I will be with you, and you will destroy the Midianites as if you were fighting against one man.'"
— *Judges 6:11–16 NLT*

Imagine someone coming up to you and saying, "Mighty hero, God is with you!" You might respond like Gideon, "Yeah, right. Look at me—I've got nothing going for me." You might even wonder, "Why would God choose someone like me after everything I've been through? After all my failures?"

It's easy to disqualify yourself, but that's exactly when God steps in. God doesn't call the qualified; He qualifies the called. When Jesus died on the cross, He didn't do it for people who had it all together. He did it for people like you and me—broken, hurting, and unsure of ourselves. When He hung on that cross, He looked at you and said, "You are worth it."

"You Are Chosen, Even When You Don't Feel It"

When I was lost, I asked myself the same question Gideon did: "How can I make a difference when I feel so weak?" But God spoke to me, just as He did to Gideon: "Go in the strength you have." God isn't looking for perfect people; He's looking for those who are willing. When Gideon doubted, God didn't leave him. He promised to go with him, and that's His promise to you too.

BREAKING THE CHAINS OF THE PAST

When God called Gideon, He instructed him to get rid of the idols in his life—the things that held him back. For many of us, those idols are tied to our past. Whether it's toxic relationships, habits, or the desire for worldly approval, these things can prevent us from stepping into the freedom God has for us. God can't use you fully until you surrender completely. Gideon had to break free from the idols of his past, and so do we.

In my own life, I had to let go of idols like lust, the pursuit of money, and living for the approval of others. I had to tear down the things that were holding me back from fully serving God. The same may be true for you. If you feel trapped by sin or stuck in the past, know this: Jesus has already won your freedom—you just need to let go of the things that are holding you captive.

LEAD WITH BOLDNESS

When the Spirit of God came upon Gideon, he was no longer the scared man hiding in a winepress. He became a bold leader who led his people to victory. God doesn't just call you—He equips you with everything you need to lead and make a difference. Like Gideon, you may be young and feel unqualified, but when God puts His seal of approval on you, nothing can stand in your way.

What would happen if the young people in today's church caught hold of this kind of boldness? What if instead of just going through the motions, we became leaders in every area—senators, entrepreneurs, artists, and influencers for the Kingdom of God? The next generation is looking for leaders, and God is calling you to step up.

DON'T LET FEAR DISQUALIFY YOU

When God trimmed down Gideon's army from 32,000 to 300, He wasn't looking for the strongest or the bravest—He was looking for those who were willing to trust Him. Fear disqualified 22,000 men from the battle. Don't let fear disqualify you from what God wants to do through you. If you let fear control your life, you will miss out on the incredible things God has prepared for you. The battle belongs to the Lord, and He will give you the victory, just as He did for Gideon.

OBEDIENCE BRINGS BREAKTHROUGH

Just like in Gideon's story, obedience is the key to victory. It may seem small, but every step of faith you take brings you closer to the breakthrough God has for you. You don't need to be perfect to be used by God, but you do need to be obedient. Disobedience leads to destruction, but obedience leads to life and purpose.

As young people, it's easy to get caught up in what the world says we should be. But when we choose to follow God, He leads us into the fullness of His plan for our lives. You are not disqualified by your past. You are chosen, and God has more in store for you than you can imagine. Step into the calling He has for you, and watch as He uses your life to deliver those around you.

THE CHALLENGE
#STEP OUT IN FAITH AND LEAD

I challenge you to take a bold step of faith in an area where you've been hesitant or felt disqualified. It could be something small or big—God honors the action. Ask God to reveal where you need to trust Him more, and then obey His leading.

- **Reflect**: Spend time in prayer asking God to reveal areas in your life where fear or past mistakes are holding you back. Write down any thoughts or feelings that come up.

- **Act**: After reflecting, identify one tangible action you can take to start breaking free from fear or feelings of inadequacy. It could be reaching out to someone for help, starting a conversation with someone who needs encouragement, serving in your community or church, or making a decision to let go of something holding you back.

- **Lead**: This week, aim to lead by example. Whether at school, work, or home, show others what it looks like to step into God's calling with courage. Don't worry about being perfect; just take the first step.

Remember Gideon: God called him a mighty hero even when he felt weak and unqualified. God is saying the same to you today. Step out in faith—He is with you!

CHAPTER 11
AGENTS OF CHANGE

And He said to them, "Go into all the world and preach the gospel to all creation. He who has believed [in me] and has been baptized will be saved [from the penalty of God's wrath and judgment]; but he who has not believed will be condemned. These signs will accompany those who have believed: in my name they will cast out demons, they will speak in new tongues; they will pick up serpents, and if they drink anything deadly, it will not hurt them; they will lay hands on the sick, and they will get well."
MARK 16:15–18 AMP

"God doesn't deal with you based on your past. He deals with you based on your future."

THE CALL TO BE AGENTS OF CHANGE

This passage isn't just an invitation but a commissioning. It's Jesus' way of empowering us to take the gospel and go beyond the familiar walls of our churches. Yet, many have read this as if it says, "Go into your church, hear the gospel, and afterward, go home to watch the Sunday football game." There's nothing wrong with football, but when our Sundays revolve around entertainment rather than encountering God, we lose touch with the mission Jesus set before us.

You weren't called to be an agent of compromise but an agent of change. When you accepted salvation, you received the entire package—a perfect redemption through Jesus' sacrifice. This calling, rooted in the Great Commission, charges us to bring hope, healing, and transformation wherever we go. As Mark 16:17 reminds us,

"These signs shall accompany them," yet today, many are seeking signs rather than living lives that cause signs to follow them. Revival isn't something we chase; as believers, we are called to walk in a way that revival chases us.

THE BENEFITS OF FAITHFUL SERVICE

"Bless and affectionately praise the Lord, O my soul, and all that is within me, bless His holy name. Bless and affectionately praise the Lord, O my soul, and do not forget any of His benefits." — Psalms 103:1 AMP

Psalm 103 provides a profound picture of the benefits of living in faith: God forgives our sins, heals our diseases, shows mercy, and satisfies us with good things. This is the inheritance of all who believe in Him. At the cross, God's mercy and redemption are available to everyone who calls upon His name. These benefits—undeserved blessings, divine forgiveness, and steadfast love—are ours to claim in every situation.

So, when life's difficulties weigh on us, remember to "forget not His benefits." These blessings are reminders of the transformative work that God has done and continues to do. When things don't go as planned, reflect on what Jesus has already accomplished for you, reminding yourself of His unchanging promise.

A PERSONAL MISSION: BECOMING AN AGENT OF CHANGE

A few years ago, as I prepared for a mission trip to Nicaragua, I felt God impress something on my heart. Late one night, He woke me, saying, "You are an agent of change; I am sending you to a desert land, but you can only bring change because I am with you." I had been fasting and praying for the people we planned to serve. We were heading to a place where families lived amid garbage, their homes made of plastic and sticks, and where a day's labor yielded only fifty cents. Here, "one man's trash" became "another man's treasure."

I questioned my ability to make any meaningful impact on this community. What could I, a seminary student with no income, possibly offer to people who had nothing? That's when I understood that the call wasn't about what I could do but about what God could do through me. By His grace, our small team of twenty-five people raised $30,000, enough to fund a soup kitchen and help those families find a pathway out of poverty.

It wasn't about our resources but our willingness. We allowed ourselves to be used by God, and He transformed lives. This mission was a testament to how God can use even the smallest group of people to bring monumental change.

YOUR CALL TO ACTION: EMBRACING THE ROLE OF AN AGENT OF CHANGE

Where is God calling you to be an agent of change? Perhaps it's in your community, your workplace, or somewhere beyond your current comfort zone. The specifics don't matter as much as the willingness to answer the call. Being an agent of change means embracing the mission of transformation, wherever that may lead. It's about being bold in faith, carrying the gospel not just in words but in action.

Remember: When you choose to say "yes" to God's call, He will equip you, empower you, and transform you. You aren't simply carrying a message; you're carrying the kingdom of God into places of darkness, bringing light and hope. God doesn't look at your past to determine your future; He sees the potential for greatness that comes from living a life committed to His purpose.

In answering the call to be an agent of change, you are stepping into a purpose greater than yourself. The world may not always recognize this calling, but God sees it, and He will be with you every step of the way. Embrace this commission, for it is the greatest adventure you can undertake.

THE VALLEY

As agents of change, we must be prepared to face opposition and endure periods of struggle—what some might call a "valley experience." But what exactly is a valley experience? It's a season when you feel isolated, vulnerable, and challenged; a place that may feel empty and overshadowed by hardship. David described it this way:

"Even though I walk through the [sunless] valley of the shadow of death, I fear no evil, for you are with me; your rod [to protect] and your staff [to guide], they comfort and console me."
— Psalm 23:4, AMP

David's words remind us that while we may journey through valleys, we are never alone. Rather than questioning why hardships come, we can choose to thank God for His unwavering presence and use this time as a period of growth. Just as a mountain's summit offers breathtaking views but sparse vegetation, growth flourishes in the valley. To bear fruit and thrive, we must journey through these low points, for it is here, in the valley, that our roots deepen.

"In those days, Jesus came from Nazareth of Galilee and was baptized by John in the Jordan River. Immediately coming up out of the water, He (John) saw the heavens torn open, and the Spirit like a dove descending on Him (Jesus); and a voice came out of heaven saying: 'You are My Beloved Son, in You I am well-pleased and delighted!' Immediately, the [Holy] Spirit forced Him out into the wilderness (desert). He was in the wilderness (desert) forty days being tempted [to do evil] by Satan; and He was with the wild animals, and the angels ministered continually to Him."
— Mark 1:9–13, ESV

Even Jesus faced His own valley experience. Directly after being filled with the Holy Spirit, He was driven into the wilderness to endure temptation and testing. Some believe that receiving the Holy Spirit brings a life of ease, but Mark's Gospel reveals otherwise. Jesus was empowered by the Spirit not to rest in comfort but to withstand hardship and temptation, all to prepare Him for His ministry. He endured the wilderness to bring hope and healing to a world in need.

As agents of change, we are called to bring life to barren places, reflecting the true meaning of "Go into all the world." This mandate isn't about reaching only the pleasant places but also the deserts of life—the dark, desolate spaces where hope is absent. God's power shines brightest in these challenging places. If you find yourself in a "desert season," take heart—you are in good company. Sometimes, the Spirit leads us through the desert to strengthen us and prepare us for greater purposes.

THE ROLE OF AGENTS OF CHANGE

The world today needs agents of change filled with the Holy Spirit who are willing to go into the world's deserts—places of hopelessness, fear, and moral decay. To transform a barren place into a flourishing garden, we must follow the example Jesus set for us: plant seeds of life one at a time, wherever we go. Our mission isn't just to attend church but to embody God's love and purpose daily. Living as an agent of change is how we help restore the world around us.

IDENTITY: KNOWING WHO YOU ARE IN CHRIST

Being an agent of change is about embodying the identity of a disciple of Jesus. Jesus chose twelve disciples, and through them, His message spread throughout the entire world. They started where they were and expanded outward, bringing the gospel to Rome, Spain, Africa, China, and beyond. They understood their identity, a clarity that empowered them to change history. In the same way, God wants you to know your identity as His disciple. This identity isn't confined to church walls; it's a way of life that permeates every day, every hour, every place you go.

Consider the story of a soldier who mistakenly received skydiving orders. Despite having no training, he followed through on the mission, saying, "I was given the papers, so I was authorized by those in authority." Like that soldier, we have been given our "orders"—God's Word. We have been commissioned by Jesus, the King of glory, to bring life to desolate areas.

"Therefore, become imitators of God [copy Him and follow His example], as well-beloved children [imitate their father]."
— Ephesians 5:1, AMP

Paul reminds us to imitate God, to approach situations with faith and resolve, bringing light into darkness just as Jesus did. Jesus said He only did what He saw the Father doing, and we are called to live with this same purpose. Our focus should shift from seeking human approval to seeking what pleases God.

CONFIDENCE IN YOUR CALLING

"For everyone born of God is victorious and overcomes the world; and this is the victory that has conquered and overcome the world—our [continuing, persistent] faith [in Jesus the Son of God]."
— 1 John 5:4, AMP

In a world that often questions the reality of miracles and divine power, we are called to reawaken this generation to the heart of the Father. By embracing our God-given identity, we unlock our potential and gain access to the supernatural promises of God. The enemy wants to keep this knowledge from us, but our faith compels us to seek and embody the purpose Jesus secured on the cross.

"In this [union and fellowship with Him], love is completed and perfected with us, so that we may have confidence in the day of judgment [with assurance and boldness to face Him]; because as He is, so are we in this world."
— 1 John 4:17, AMP

Just as Jesus healed, forgave, and provided hope, so are we empowered to do the same in this world. John's words are a powerful reminder: we are called to continue Jesus' work here and now. If we long to see God's results, we must fully embrace this identity and carry His love into every interaction, every environment, every challenge we encounter.

THE CALL

As a born-again believer, you hold a special role as an ambassador of God's Kingdom on earth. Your mission, as an "agent of change," is to establish His Kingdom here. Just as the United States assigns ambassadors to nearly every country, representing its values and authority, so are we appointed as representatives of Christ. Ambassadors are chosen because they embody the nation they serve, and in the same way, we are chosen to reflect Christ. This position isn't about qualifications we bring but about His selection and provision. In choosing us, God has already equipped us for this purpose, though not everyone is actively responding to the call.

"To be an agent of change, you must be chosen." As John 15:16 (AMP) says, "You have not chosen me, but I had chosen you and appointed and purposefully planted you so that you would go and bear fruit and keep on bearing... so that whatever you ask of the Father in my name [as My representative] He may give to you." Before we were born, God had this calling in place. Don't let the lie that you're "not good enough" hold you back; God's calling comes with His provision.

We are equipped with powerful spiritual weapons, not just physical or human resources. "The weapons of our warfare are not physical [weapons of flesh and blood]," as 2 Corinthians 10:4-5 (AMP) states. They are divinely powerful for overcoming challenges that block God's truth. Our fight is against forces greater than the people or obstacles we see; it's a spiritual battle against the schemes of Satan, who aims to steal, kill, and destroy (John 10:10). We cannot combat these spiritual issues alone. Through faith and prayer, we give God full authority to act, aligning with His promise in Isaiah 54:17 (AMP): "No weapon that is formed against you will succeed..."

Just as every military force operates under the guidance of a commander, we too, in God's army, follow His lead through the Holy Spirit. The Spirit is our Counselor and Helper, whom Jesus sent to guide and empower us (John 14:16-17, AMP). It's crucial to maintain a close relationship with Jesus, moving beyond one sermon a week to daily discipline, meditating on His Word and listening for His will.

Many miss this guidance and follow the "permissible" will rather than the "perfect" will of God, which calls for obedience to the Spirit's voice. God already has a plan for each of us, as Psalm 139:16 reveals. We are to let the Spirit lead us as we study and pray, allowing Him to direct our steps toward being agents of change as Jesus was.

Jesus promised that we, as His representatives, would do "greater works" in His name (John 14:12-13, AMP). This isn't about striving or striving to measure up; rather, it's allowing Christ in us—the hope of glory—to manifest through us. When I began working in the foster care system, I wanted each child I met to experience healing and God's love. Through simple acts of love and living out the Word, I saw lives change. Some kids, noticing a difference in me, would ask, "Why are you different?" It gave me the chance to reflect Jesus to them.

Not all have accepted Christ yet, but that doesn't deter me from praying and prophesying over them. Some may see it as foolish, wondering why anyone would invest in "hopeless" lives. But I know the power of God to transform. As someone who once relied on the unwavering prayers of a loved one, I now stand in the gap for these kids. Where there's brokenness, I believe God's light shines brightest. So, let's remember that while the world may deem it impossible, with God, all things are possible.

AGENTS OF CHANGE ON THE RISE

Let's consider marriage as an illustration of authority. When my wife took my last name, she inherited all that I am and have; she could walk into the bank and access any of my accounts. Why? Because by taking my name, she gained full access and authority. In a similar way, the Bible tells us:

> *"And there is salvation in no one else; for there is no other name under heaven that has been given among people by which we must be saved [for God has provided the world no alternative for salvation]."*
> —Acts 4:12 (AMP)

The name of Jesus wasn't given to simply record in history but to actively use as a powerful force. The sheer impact of His name goes beyond what we can fully comprehend. In Acts 3, we find Peter and John, heading to the temple for prayer, encountering a man crippled since birth. Each day, people passed this man, set at the temple gate called Beautiful, as he begged for money. For forty years, he remained in the same spot, largely ignored by those who claimed to follow God—a scene not unlike what we often see today. We can become so absorbed in our routines, programs, and even technology that we miss those around us in need.

Consider a modern story of a pastor who tested his church's heart by dressing as a homeless man. Sitting outside the church, he watched as members entered without offering help or acknowledgment. When the new pastor was finally introduced, he walked to the front, still in disguise, and said, "We have a lot of work to do here." Then he dismissed the congregation, leaving a powerful impression. This incident starkly reminded the congregation—and us—that sometimes we pass by the very people we are meant to help.

Returning to Acts 3, many who passed by that crippled man were unaware of the power within them. They'd heard of miracles and healings but didn't realize they could be a part of them. Even today, many churchgoers believe only pastors can pray for the sick. We often fail to act because we don't grasp the authority we carry as followers of Jesus.

But when Peter and John arrived, everything changed. When the man asked for money, they responded with something far greater. Peter said, "Silver and gold I do not have; but what I do have I give to you: In the name (authority, power) of Jesus Christ the Nazarene—walk and go on walking!" (Acts 3:6 AMP). Peter and John knew they were acting under the command of the Holy Spirit, fully aware of the authority in Jesus' name. The man expected something when he looked at them—and expectation is key. What are your expectations when you use the name of Jesus? Are you ready to witness the God of miracles? This is what being an agent of change is all about—showing the world that God is alive and powerful.

When Peter declared, "In the name of Jesus, rise up and walk," he unlocked healing, freedom, and restoration through that powerful name. In the same way, declare over your life: "In the name of Jesus, my addictions are broken. In the name of Jesus, every chain the enemy has placed on me is released. In the name of Jesus, healing flows, and lack turns to abundance." Speak this over yourself, your family, and those you love who may feel crippled by life's challenges.

The name of Jesus is given to us as agents of change, to bring healing to the sick, freedom to the oppressed, and peace to the fearful. This generation needs you to rise as a beacon of hope. I may not have silver or gold, but what I do have, I give to you: in the name of Jesus of Nazareth—walk! Walk into your purpose, your calling, your God-given assignment, and His perfect will for you. Amen.

THE CHALLENGE
#INVITE A GROUP OF FRIENDS TO GO OUT TO SHARE THE GOSPEL

I am not ashamed of the Gospel, for it is the power of God for salvation [from His wrath and punishment] to everyone who believes [in Christ as Savior], to the Jew first and also to the Greek.
ROMANS 1:16 AMP

One day in college, I was spending time with friends, and our conversation turned to how broken the world seemed. We realized that instead of just talking about the problems, we could take action and share hope. So, we decided to go to the mall and see if God would lead us to people who needed to hear the Gospel. We paired up and walked through the mall, praying that God would show us whom to speak with.

I noticed a young man sitting alone, looking visibly stressed. I couldn't just pass by; I felt a strong urge to talk to him. I approached him and simply said, "Hey man, I just want you to know Jesus loves you." Instantly, he started to cry. Caught off guard, I listened as he shared that he'd just been dropped off by his father, who wanted nothing more to do with him after a difficult court case that morning. I had the opportunity to encourage him, share the hope of Jesus, and ultimately lead him to faith. That moment taught me that sharing your faith doesn't require special talents—just a willing heart. Jesus takes care of the rest.

That day, several people experienced the love of God through my friends and me, and a couple of them even accepted Christ. This experience showed me that anyone can make a difference if they're willing to give God just one afternoon and share the Good News with others. You and your friends can also become agents of change, seizing every opportunity to bring hope to the world around you.

CHAPTER 12
UNLEASHING YOUR POTENTIAL

When a soldier first enlists in the Army, he is asked, "Why do you want to be a part of the Army?" The motivation behind this commitment is often a sense of duty and the awareness of a need. This sense of need should also drive every believer to move from merely attending church to actively living out their faith. Accepting Jesus is not a membership to a club but an enlistment to an assignment. Yet, in many churches, new believers are handed membership cards, unintentionally shifting them into a passive "club" mindset rather than a mission-minded life.

This distinction is critical: a membership club offers perks and entertainment, but being part of God's rescue mission means you're called to action. Statistics show that in most churches, only 20 percent of members are actively engaged, and only a fraction of them know their purpose. Meanwhile, the remaining 80 percent are passive spectators, unaware of the powerful role they're meant to play in God's Kingdom. Many leaders hesitate to address this issue, but this 80 percent is the missing link to true revival. When 100 percent of God's people cry out with hunger for Him, revival will follow, shaking the heavens. But God won't move fully until all His people are prepared and engaged for this final mission.

A GENERATION WITHOUT ASSIGNMENT

In 1 Kings, we see Solomon growing up under David's leadership, knowing he'd one day carry on his father's work. Before David died, he charged Solomon with this responsibility:

"I am about to go the way of all the earth. So be strong, act like a man, and observe what the Lord your God requires: Walk in obedience to Him, keep His

decrees and commands, His laws and regulations, as written in the Law of Moses. Do this so that you may prosper in all you do and wherever you go."
—1 Kings 2:2-3 (AMP)

David prepared Solomon for leadership, but Solomon only truly stepped into his role when he took ownership of his assignment. The reason many believers remain passive is that they haven't embraced their place in the body of Christ. Many don't realize they've been called by God Himself. But I want to remind you today: everyone around you has a purpose.

In 1 Corinthians 12, Paul addresses spiritual gifts in the church at Corinth, where, again, only 20 percent were active in their divine assignments, while 80 percent remained spectators. Paul urged them to engage, saying, "The manifestation of the Spirit is given to each one for the profit of all." Recognize this: if you take nothing else from today, know that you are called by God Himself. Scripture says, "Whosoever believes." Are you part of that "whosoever"? I am, and so are you.

Jesus affirmed this calling in John 15:16 (AMP): "You have not chosen me, but I have chosen you and appointed you to go and bear fruit, fruit that will last…" You are chosen for a purpose. The Israelites wandered in the wilderness for forty years—a journey that could have taken only days—because only 20 percent were actively following God's leading, while the rest murmured and complained. If each person had recognized their assignment, they could have all supported Moses and walked together in power and unity. But doubt and distraction kept them from walking in their purpose—and the promise. Your promise is tied to your assignment. The reward of the promise comes as you walk in and complete the purpose God has set for you. Just as the Israelites were tasked with driving out the inhabitants of the land God promised, your blessing is connected to fulfilling your God-given mission. If they had abandoned their assignment, there would be no promised land. Likewise, the fulfillment of your promise is directly linked to you stepping into your divine assignment.

How Do You Find Your Assignment?

Paul explained that the body of Christ is made up of many parts, each with a unique role. He said, "If the foot should say, 'Because I am not a hand, I do not belong to the body,' it would not for that reason cease to be part of the body." Many people feel they have "nothing to offer" and doubt their place. But remember, being a part of the church body isn't about feeling qualified; it's about knowing you belong. Like a soldier who discovers his role through training, you were born with an assignment, and the challenges you face help you develop the resilience needed to fulfill it.

"Every trial, difficulty, and battle in your life is preparation for your assignment."

While some struggles come from resisting God's guidance, God can transform even our mistakes into valuable lessons for our mission. For example, I once struggled with addiction. My own choices brought pain, but now, God uses my past to reach others struggling with the same issue. Every difficult experience can equip you to guide others toward God's purpose for them.

Paul goes on to say, "If the ear should say, 'Because I am not an eye, I do not belong to the body,' it would not cease to be part of the body." Each of us is placed in the body by God's design, uniquely equipped to serve His purpose:

"But now, God has placed and arranged the parts in the body, each one of them, just as He willed and saw fit."
—1 Corinthians 12:16–18 (AMP)

God has already set your role, and behind every assignment, He has prepared deliverance and provision. When God called Abraham, He'd already prepared his path:

> *"The Lord said to Abram, 'Go from your country, your people, and your father's household to the land I will show you. I will make you into a great nation, and I will bless you.'"*
> *—Genesis 12:1–2 (AMP)*

For Abraham, stepping into his assignment meant walking in faith, not questioning God's direction. Like Abraham, we don't choose our assignments; God ordains them. Many today aren't fulfilling their purpose because they're waiting for the "right" assignment rather than accepting the one God has given them. This is why so many fall away—they're trying to walk in their own strength instead of relying on God's provision and grace for His assignment. Fear keeps 80 percent from leaving their "Egypt." To discover your assignment, you must let go and trust God, even if past wounds and failures have left you cautious.

> *"Arise [from spiritual depression to a new life], shine [be radiant with the glory and brilliance of the Lord]; for your light has come, and the glory of the Lord has risen upon you."*
> *—Isaiah 60:1 (AMP)*

Spiritual discouragement keeps many from living out their calling. God invites you to rise above the past and walk in His light, where He has already made a path for you. Dare to believe, step out in faith, and embrace the new thing He wants to do through you:

> *"Do not remember the former things, or ponder the things of the past. Listen carefully, I am about to do a new thing; now it will spring forth. I will even put a road in the wilderness, rivers in the desert."*
> *—Isaiah 43:18–19 (ESV)*

Finding your assignment starts with letting go of the past, trusting God's leading, and stepping into the new things He has prepared.

Do not remember the former things, or ponder the things of the past.

Listen carefully, I am about to do a new thing, Now it will spring forth; will you not be aware of it? I will even put a road in the wilderness, Rivers in the desert.
ISAIAH 43:18–19 ESV

THE DANGERS OF DISTRACTIONS FROM YOUR ASSIGNMENT

King Solomon loved many foreign women, including the daughter of Pharaoh, despite God's command to Israel not to associate with nations that would lead them astray. Yet Solomon clung to these women in love, amassing 700 wives and 300 concubines, who eventually turned his heart away from God. In his old age, Solomon's devotion wavered, and he strayed from his father David's wholehearted commitment to the Lord.
—*1 Kings 11:1–4 (AMP)*

Solomon understood his assignment. He had initially asked God for wisdom to lead Israel well:
"So give your servant an understanding heart to judge Your people, that I may discern between good and evil."
—*1 Kings 3:9 (AMP)*

God was pleased with Solomon's request, and He's pleased when we see a need and respond. Meeting a need often leads us directly to our God-given assignment. While many wait for a clear sign, God's heart is for those who are willing to act now. The need for compassion is all around us—the widows, the homeless, the young who need hope—and God won't wait for us forever. When you make the needs around you part of your mission, God will bless and expand your reach. Solomon's commitment led him to wealth and wisdom beyond measure. Fulfilling your assignment can elevate you to places of influence.

But the enemy works to derail us from our assignments. Solomon's relationships ultimately led him away from God's purposes, drawing him into idol worship despite starting out with great devotion. What distractions are keeping you from your calling? Relationships, depression, temptations, disappointments—all can pull you away from the path God has for you. Jesus understood His purpose from an early age and focused entirely on fulfilling the Father's will, knowing that His assignment was not self-directed but God-given.

Jesus said, "I do not seek my own will, but the will of Him who sent me."
—John 5:30 (AMP)

Today, people struggle with finding their purpose, often distracted by personal desires rather than seeking God's direction. Our "selfie" culture fuels self-centered ambitions that can leave us disconnected from God's true assignment for us.

DON'T LOSE YOUR ASSIGNMENT

The Lord warned Solomon: "Because you have done this and not kept My covenant, I will tear the kingdom away from you and give it to your servant."
—1 Kings 11:11 (ESV)

Solomon's story is a cautionary tale. He began with zeal and wisdom but ended his life out of alignment with God's will, leading to the loss of everything he'd worked for. Losing your assignment affects every part of your life—relationships, family, ministry, and opportunities to impact others. Without God's direction, we end up pursuing only what seems right to us.

Paul spoke to this challenge and shared the foundation for staying on course:

"Earnestly desire the greater gifts. And I will show you a more excellent way…unselfish love."
—1 Corinthians 12:31 (AMP)

Ultimately, love is our highest calling. Love keeps us grounded, guides us through the challenges of our assignments, and empowers us to complete them. Without love, we're merely making noise. Walk in love, and you'll find the strength and focus needed to fulfill the purpose God has given you.

THIS GENERATION NEEDS YOUR ASSIGNMENT

Our society's decline is due in part to the 80 percent of Christians who, instead of serving in their God-given assignments, have become passive. Many were meant to guide struggling teenagers, bring hope to the suicidal, or provide stability for families. Countless men were called to raise their children with their wives, and many women were called to nurture life, but when people neglect their assignments, it creates a ripple effect that fosters brokenness.

The issues we face today—like the normalization of abortion, corruption, sexual immorality, addiction, and lukewarm faith—stem from people abandoning their purpose. However, it's possible to return to God's design, one person at a time, by fulfilling one need at a time. This is how the early church in Acts operated, and their impact was astonishing:

> *"Now the company of believers was of one heart and soul, and not one [of them] claimed that anything belonging to him was [exclusively] his own, but everything was common property and for the use of all. And with great ability and power, the apostles were continuously testifying to the resurrection of the Lord Jesus, and great grace [God's remarkable loving kindness and favor and goodwill] rested richly upon them all. There was not a needy person among them..."*
> —Acts 4:32–35 (AMP)

This is the power of a generation living in alignment with their assignments. They recognized their purpose and served together in unity.

PROPHETIC WORD

By the Spirit of the Living God, this generation will rise to fulfill its assignment:

> *"And it shall be in the last days, says the Lord,*
> *That I will pour out my Spirit upon all mankind;*
> *And your sons and your daughters shall prophesy,*
> *And your young men shall see [divinely prompted] visions,*
> *And your old men shall dream [divinely prompted] dreams."*
> —Joel 2:28 (AMP)

To every person reading this, I pray this prophetic word takes root in your life and that the Holy Spirit brings its meaning alive in you. Young people will dream of God's heart and proclaim it boldly. Those with a vision will see it clearly and declare it in Jesus' name. The elderly will dream of what God is set to do in these last days, with divine interpretations to share.

As each generation embraces its assignment, the glory of God will fill the earth.

THE GAP FILLER

> *"By this everyone will know that you are my disciples, if you have love and unselfish concern for one another."*
> —John 13:35 (ESV)

Throughout this book, we've explored how to become agents of change. Jesus, during His time on earth, had one primary mission: to bridge the gap between a broken generation and God's love. This same call extends to us today—to become a bridge of hope, stepping away from judgment and pointing fingers, and instead embracing a life of service, love, and compassion.

As we face a world filled with loneliness, depression, addiction, and division, Jesus asks us to "fill the gap" through love. Our culture doesn't need more accusations; it needs genuine, sacrificial love. This kind of love means putting others first, as Jesus instructed:

> *"'You shall love the Lord your God with all your heart, soul, and mind... and love your neighbor as yourself.'"*
> —Matthew 22:37–39 (AMP)

Jesus exemplified this by living out love in every interaction. Today, this challenge remains: can we genuinely love our neighbor as ourselves, not just in words but through action? The early church in Acts set an example, sharing resources selflessly and fulfilling each other's needs. When we live this way, we strengthen the "curtain rod" that holds God's blessings for our lives; without it, our faith and blessings falter.

Our society's transformation depends on believers stepping into this role as gap-fillers. Every time we withhold love or compassion, we create space for darkness. But with love, we embody God's promise and His light for others. God's covenant with us is unchanging; even when we fall, He is faithful. Our role is to live out this love in action, becoming vessels of healing and reconciliation in a world that desperately needs it.

A LIFE OF LOVE IN ACTION

Jesus' message is clear: if we claim to love God, we must love others, not only in words but with genuine, practical acts of compassion. Without this love, we cannot truly reflect His light. As the Apostle John warns, "If anyone says, 'I love God,' and hates his brother, he is a liar" (1 John 4:20 AMP). Our call is simple yet powerful: live a life of love, meet needs where we see them, and be a reflection of Jesus to a world in need. Are you willing to be the gap filler in this generation?

> *But Jesus replied, of God "It is written and forever remains written, 'Man shall not live by bread alone, but by every word that comes out of the mouth.'"*
> MATTHEW 4:4 ESV

JESUS SAID

Follow me, and I will make you fishers of men.
MATTHEW 4:19 ESV

This meant He doesn't just want you to be saved, but to go get those around you who are drowning. Ninety-five percent of Christians have never won a soul for the Lord according to statistics.

Let your light shine before men so that they may glorify your father in Heaven: meaning do good to others that is the only way the light will shine.
MATTHEW 5:16 ESV

But I say unto you that whoever is angry with his brother without cause shall be in danger of judgment.
MATHEW 5:22 ESV

Therefore if you bring your gift to the altar and there remember that you have something against your brother leave your gift there before the altar and go and reconciled with your neighbor first and then come and give your gift.
MATTHEW 5:24 ESV

How many times have we helped charities, given to the poor, or given at a church when we were in offense against our neighbor? Those things did not count because we were in a state of being out of Love.

But I say unto you do not resist an evil person but whoever strikes you at your right cheek turn to him the other as well.
MATTHEW 5:39 ESV

You have heard that it was said, "You shall love your neighbor [fellow man] and hate your enemy." But I say to you, love [that is, unselfishly seek the best or higher good for] your enemies and pray for those who persecute you, so that you may [show yourselves to] be the children of your Father who is in heaven; for He makes His sun rise on those who are evil and on those who are good, and makes the rain fall on the

righteous [those who are morally upright] and the unrighteous [the unrepentant, those who oppose Him]. For if you love [only] those who love you, what reward do you have? Do not even the tax collectors do that? And if you greet only your brothers [wishing them God's blessing and peace], what more [than others] are you doing? Do not even the Gentiles [who do not know the Lord] do that? You, therefore, will be perfect [growing into spiritual maturity both in mind and character, actively integrating godly values into your daily life], as your heavenly Father is perfect.
MATTHEW 5:43–48 ESV

For if you forgive man their sins your heavenly father will forgive you. But if you do not forgive men for their sins, neither will your heavenly father forgive you.
MATTHEW 6:14 ESV

Judge not that you be not judged. For with the judgment you judged you will be judged.
MATTHEW 7:1–2 ESV

Everything you would like man to do unto you, do also for them, for this is the law of the prophets.
MATTHEW 7:12 ESV

Those whom are well do not need a physician but I came for those who are sick to save them.
MATTHEW 9:12 ESV

Whoever gives even a cup to this little ones of mine, truly I tell you he shall receive a reward.
MATTHEW 10:42 ESV

The son of Man did not come to be served but to serve and to give his life as a ransom for many.
MATTHEW 20:28 ESV

Depart from me you cursed into eternal fire, for I was hungry and you gave me no food, I was thirsty and you gave me no drink, I was a

> *stranger and you did not take me in, I was naked and you did not clothe me, I was sick and in prison and you did not visit me. Then they will ask me Lord when did we see you hungry or thirsty or a stranger or naked or sick or in prison and did not serve you? Then I will say truly I say to you as you did it not for one of the least of these you did it not for me. And they will go away into eternal punishment, but the righteous into eternal life.*
> MATTHEW 25:41 ESV

What excuse do we have today? These verses reveal our responsibility as agents of change in this generation. They challenge us to live out unconditional love for our neighbor—love that doesn't depend on convenience or comfort. Take time to meditate on them, let them transform your heart, and your life will never be the same. For too long, we've been absorbed in self-interest, but it's time to leave the "selfie generation" behind and embrace God's calling to love beyond ourselves.

In Matthew 28, Jesus gave us the Great Commission: to go out and love our neighbors with agape love. We have seen the consequences of ignoring this command. Racism, division, and judgment are rooted in the absence of love, yet Jesus instructed us to "go into the entire world" to spread His love without conditions. Instead, our purpose has drifted. Sunday mornings in America remain the most segregated time of the week—Baptists with Baptists, Pentecostals with Pentecostals. Where is God's love in this picture? Where is the unity that He demonstrated here on earth?

For years, we have loved conditionally, creating a gap between God and humanity. When we say, "I love you with the love of Christ," it must mean more than words—it should reflect love without limits, a love that doesn't keep a record of wrongs but leads to true surrender. This is the change we need today.

Let this prayer begin our journey:
"God, I admit I can't love my neighbor as I should. But because of Your love for me, and by Your grace, I choose to forgive those who have hurt me and those closest to me. Today, I forgive them in Jesus'

name."

Our aim must be to love on purpose: even when wronged, we respond with love. When gossiped about, we choose love. Even when hurt, we give agape love at all costs.

"By this, everyone will know that you are my disciples if you have love and unselfish concern for one another."
—John 13:35 (ESV)

Let's go out and be the change.

THE CHALLENGE
#TAKE A STEP OF FAITH IN YOUR GOD ASSIGNMENT

For His anger is but for a moment,
His favor is for a lifetime.
Weeping may endure for a night
but a shout of joy comes in the morning.
PSALMS 30:5 AMP

This final challenge is about finding and stepping into your assignment. My prayer is that the truth of this message becomes a revelation in your life. This challenge is for those who know God has called them but who, due to fear, haven't yet taken the leap of faith. Some of you reading this have felt the Lord calling you to step out, yet you've stayed on the boat, uncertain of how things will unfold. This call is for you—entrepreneurs, future ministers, those called to serve in their local church, young preachers, and anyone who hasn't yet surrendered fully to Christ. Now is the time to step forward. No more wandering in the wilderness; it's time to move toward your promised land. Follow Jesus' leading and allow the Holy Spirit to guide your steps.

We cannot afford to wait any longer. Each unfulfilled assignment is a piece of what this generation needs to rise as a godly influence. If each of us moved forward in our calling, we would fill the gaps needed to cultivate a better, God-centered society. Consider those who sing secular songs about fame, indulgence, and fleeting pleasure. Many of today's popular artists—like Beyoncé, Katy Perry, and Justin Bieber—were raised in church. Their talents were intended to glorify God, yet their gifts have been redirected. This is why it's essential that we remain focused on our calling. Step out in faith, trusting God to guide you in fulfilling the assignment He's given you. Your obedience today will influence the generation of tomorrow.

YOUR STORY MATTERS

You Are the Answer to Our Generation

Yet in all these things we are more than conquerors and gain an overwhelming victory through Him who loved us [so much that He died for us].
ROMANS 8:37 AMP

This book was inspired by a deep awareness that we are created as God's children to be more than conquerors. I meet people every day who feel overwhelmed by life, trapped in cycles of struggle, or searching for an escape from habits that hold them back. I've asked myself—and now I ask you—if we are born again, redeemed by Jesus, should our lives look like defeat? Do we wake up feeling unworthy, facing trials alone, while knowing we have a loving Father ready to help? My prayer is that as you read this book, you discover you were created by Almighty God for more than you can imagine. We are, indeed, more than conquerors.

When people say they know Jesus, my question is not, "Do you know Him?" but, "Does He know you?" Are you walking in a real relationship with God, or just following religion? In a true relationship, we know each other deeply; we sense when something is wrong, and we are there for each other. Many lose their true identity because they haven't spent time with the One who knows them best. That's where this book was born: in the realization that we were meant to be conquerors in Christ Jesus.

Never underestimate the power of your story—it's a testament to the transforming power of Jesus. My father always said, "You become what you say and think you are." Scripture echoes this:

"A man's [moral] self shall be filled with the fruit of his mouth, and with the consequence of his words he must be satisfied [whether good or evil]. Death and life are in the power of the tongue, and they who indulge in it shall eat the fruit of it [for death or life]." You see, you will eat the fruit of your mouth.

PROVERBS 18:20–21 AMP

ABOUT THE AUTHOR

Growing up, I never imagined I'd be doing what I am today. Raised in the Dominican Republic, I was introduced to church but felt it wasn't for me. I didn't think I could ever live up to God's standards. This led me to chase fulfillment elsewhere, making choices that brought pain instead of purpose. After years of addiction, crime, and self-destruction, a near-death experience was my wake-up call. In that moment, I turned to Jesus, asked for forgiveness, and experienced transformation. He took away my addictions, restored my family relationships, and gave me a new life. Now, I'm a changed man, walking in the identity Christ has given me—a mighty man of valor. Your story may differ, but everyone has a story. Every trial you face can become a stepping stone toward victory, making you a conqueror in Christ.

MOVING FORWARD IN FAITH

I want to thank you for joining me on this journey. My hope is that through these pages, regardless of your background, you realize that God is calling you to be part of His Kingdom. Will you commit with me to being part of His Church, His body, until He returns?

"If you acknowledge and confess with your mouth that Jesus is Lord [recognizing His power, authority, and majesty as God], and believe in your heart that God raised Him from the dead, you will be saved."
—*Romans 10:9 (AMP)*

Salvation is the most precious gift offered to all who choose to acknowledge Jesus as Lord and Savior. If you feel a need to recommit your life to Jesus, do it today. You are, and always have been, His beloved creation. Invite the Lord into your heart. You don't need a church to say this prayer but you need one to build your faith in God, you also don't need to be perfect; just come as you are. God will take care of the rest.

"Jesus, I ask You today to come and make Your home in my heart. I have wandered from Your perfect plan, but I am returning to my Father's house. Forgive my sins. I declare You as Lord over my life and every decision I make. Thank You for the peace that surpasses understanding." Amen.

Welcome to the family of God!

CIVIL WAR GENERATION

OUR MISSION
AZAEL NUNEZ EVANGELISTIC MINISTRIES EXISTS TO
AWAKEN THE GENERATIONS TO BELIEVE AND WALK IN THEIR TRUE IDENTITY
AS CONQUERORS IN CHRIST JESUS.

INVITE ANEM:
AZAEL@AZAELNUNEZ.ORG

 @ANEMNETWORK

 WWW.FACEBOOK.COM/JESUSANEM

 WWW.AZAELNUNEZ.ORG

Made in the USA
Middletown, DE
07 December 2024